More Praise for *Chuck It*

"This book presents crucial advice to help managers and their staff reach the pinnacle of success in today's often ruthless and unforgiving global economy."
—Bud Hunter, vice chairman of the board, Service Corporation International (SCI)

"Nechtem proposes solutions to the most common business problems. He shows you how to make your business leaner and more competitive, while proving how to be more efficient day after day."
—Meme Omogbai, deputy director of finance and administration, the Newark Museum

"Nechtem's advice is so viable that you could implement some of his suggestions this afternoon and start seeing results first thing tomorrow morning."
—Samuel Scott, CEO, Corn Products International

"Convincingly argued and undeniably important, *Chuck It* is one of those rare mind-altering books that marks the turning point in business ethics, etiquette and in life."
—Wayne Draeger, CFO, Cummins Metropower, Inc.

"In this memoir, you can see Nechtem's equal passion for both business and people. The book proves that an emotionally healthy company is also the most productive and efficient company."
—Bruce O'Donnell, human resources manager, Catholic Charities Diocese of Metuchen

CHUCK IT

THE REVOLUTIONARY PATH TO SUCCESS AND HAPPINESS

CHUCK IT

THE REVOLUTIONARY PATH TO SUCCESS AND HAPPINESS

Chuck Nechtem

Jane Street Press

Chuck It: The Revolutionary Path to Success and Happiness
Copyright © 2008 Chuck Nechtem
Published by Jane Street Press

All rights reserved. No part of this book may be reproduced (except for inclusion in reviews), disseminated or utilized in any form or by any means, electronic or mechanical, including photocopying, recording, or in any information storage and retrieval system, or the Internet/World Wide Web without written permission from the author or publisher.

This book is intended for a general audience, does not purport to give legal advice and is not intended as a substitute for professional assistance and therefore no individual should undertake the recommendations contained herein without careful study and critical consideration. The author and publisher make no warranties or representation as to the effectiveness of the suggestions contained herein for specific readers and their specific situations. Because no two situations may be the same, and it is recommended to always consult with professionals. The publisher and author disclaim any responsibility for adverse affects resulting directly or indirectly from information contained herein.

For further information, please contact:
www.chuckitbook.com

Book design by
Arbor Books, Inc.
www.arborbooks.com

Printed in Canada

Chuck It: The Revolutionary Path to Success and Happiness
Chuck Nechtem
1. Title 2. Author 3. Motivational/Business

LCCN: 2007906551

ISBN10: 0-9799150-1-5
ISBN13: 978-0-9799150-1-7

This book is dedicated to all who read it, become more aware and take action

And for my sister, Ann

Contents

Introduction x
Finding Your Own Inspiration 1
Finding Your Own Way 7
Life in the City 13
Changing Your Path 19
Being Bold 23
Making Some Sacrifices 27
Meeting a Need 31
Persevere… 37
…and Break Through 43
Improving Self-Esteem 49
The Self-Esteem Gap 55
Fighting Dis-ease 63
How We Can Help 67
The Third Act 79
Making Choices 82
Chucking Fear 97
Life Has Its Own Hum 103
Finding the Quiet Spaces 109
A Business Plan for the New Millennium 117
A Passion Quest 131
Be a Poet in Your Business 139
Your Mission 147
Chuck's Rules 151

Introduction

It seems everywhere readers look these days, they're presented with business models, as every successful CEO opts to share his or her (usually highly sanitized) version of what made him or her a success. The public appetite for such tomes is understandable. We're a nation, after all, with a cultural work ethic that values vision, effort, status and most of all, financial gain. In business, money is how we keep score, and even in professional sports, we are as attuned to the financial statistics of our favorite athletes as we are to their batting averages or completion percentages.

The public also loves stories that offer a shortcut to a good life, whether it's better retention, a revolutionary business model or a slimmed physique. We're also a nation that, despite our Calvinist work ethic and need to excel, is always searching for The Great Hidden Thing That Will Change Everything. There are business books that offer as much, portending great fortune to those who may disregard the conventional wisdom as long as they know The Great Hidden Thing. After all, who can resist the allure of getting something for nothing?

My advice to this business philosophy is: Chuck It! This is not that kind of book. Few things in life are free or easy, and there's no miracle substitute for effort and perseverance.

Chuck It: The Revolutionary Path to Success and Happiness is the story of how I made my way in the world, both personally and professionally. There are no blueprints to success here, because every individual is different, and every situation presents a fresh set of circumstances. But this is a guide to making choices that add value to our lives, and it's also a guide to constructing a business model that operates on principles of personal integrity and providing genuine value to your customers, and providing access to success for people at every level of society. Paths to success vary with the individual. There are no universal steps.

But there are universal principles for conducting one's life as a constructive, principled and empathetic individual. Having faith in a vision and persevering despite adversity are hallmarks of successful businesspeople; using those life lessons to create a personal ethos and business environment that benefits everyone, from the CEO to the employees to the clients and yes, inevitably the stockholders, is the second part of the equation.

And learning to Chuck It, to vigorously discard those things in your life that hold you back, is an important part of achieving your full potential as a business person, and as a human being. Understanding ourselves, our strengths and weaknesses, and how we can best proceed and succeed in the world, leads to a better understanding of humanity in general.

Remember, a personal lesson learned but not applied to others' lives is an opportunity lost.

Do you have preconceived notions about your capabilities, about how other people think, about how the world works in general? Has your approach gotten you where you want to be in life?

Then Chuck It! And let's start from the beginning…

Chapter One
Finding Your Own Inspiration

Being Present

All life is a poem,
All life is a moment.

The clock ticks.
This is it.
This is it.

My own beginning wasn't auspicious. I was born in Chelsea, Massachusetts, at the time a working class area outside Boston, to parents who verbally fought all the time. It's important to understand that none of us can control our upbringing; from birth, we place our faith in the people raising us to make us feel safe and wanted. That this doesn't happen is beyond our control, but how we counter that early negative imprinting is within our control.

Even when I was very small, I knew the yelling wasn't right, and when I was a kid, all my parents did was yell, at each other and at my sister and me. Either the yelling was about having no money, living in the lower income housing projects or my sister, who was seven years older than me and couldn't seem to meet the proper boy. Why would my sister have brought a nice boy home? No one wanted to come to Chelsea, let alone project housing.

The chronic yelling is my enduring memory of childhood.

I can remember my mother using soapy water and a hand towel to wash the hallway outside our apartment because it smelled of urine. My sister had a date, and my mother was hoping to clean up the place a bit and make a good impression, but first impressions are far deeper than the cleanliness of the building.

It didn't help the emotional environment when my father mistakenly went across the street to call another woman on the phone and dialed our number by mistake, and my mother answered the phone.

"Hello, Sylvia," he said. Unfortunately, my mother's name was Evelyn. She started screaming, of course. Such incidents just increased the already high level of volatility and tension in my house.

My mom was always very depressed, which probably was worsened by the several miscarriages she had before my sister's birth. When my sister was born, there wasn't much information on postpartum depression; it was just something women had to deal with on their own, and my mother's long-term depression clearly affected my sister, who always felt it was her responsibility to take care of my mom and dad. As a result of not being able to let go emotionally, my sister developed an obsessive compulsive disorder; she couldn't let go literally. She would touch everything several times, as though making sure it was safe to pick it up.

People made light of it and called it the "double touchies," but in retrospect, she was chronically unable to let go in the figurative and psychological sense.

Even as a small boy, I somehow knew my sister's behavior wasn't right. Generally, children accept whatever is happening in their environment as the norm, but I was very aware that my sister was in pain, and I somehow knew that healthy adults came from children who had been made to feel secure and loved. No one did anything to help her, which was sad to observe, but I think my parents were too caught up in their own unhappiness to notice. And children have no place to run, because they depend on their parents to love each other and make the world secure. So even though we knew our parents cared for us, the harm they did with their behavior and the troubling behavior they ignored in my sister was quite unhealthy.

The message they sent to both of us was that world was not a safe place. Many people are given that message as children. Some never outrun that feeling.

With my mom's depression, my father being out most of the time, the lack of money and the chronic tension at home, there was very little buffering from his bad moods. I must have had good survival instincts from a young age, because I couldn't wait, even as early as my kindergarten admission, to somehow escape, to run away. I was thrilled to be out of the house for kindergarten, but I could've been going anywhere other than my house.

My sister was stuck by her psychological trauma, but being born seven years later, I wasn't afflicted to the same degree; the intensity toward me was less. And I was able to see with more clarity than my sister the impossibility of the situation, and it made me want to run away.

I think being the second child in my family was also helpful for me because I was always in the position of being the observer. I watched my mother's behavior, how her loneliness and depression affected her and everyone she came into contact with, and how her insecurity would prompt her to creep up the stairs and listen to my sister's telephone calls, as though something bad was going to happen as a result of my sister's behavior. At that time, I didn't know why she did this, and as I got older, I even tried to make her stop this intruding behavior, but I had no results. As a result, I sometimes felt like I was the junior daddy in the house, in a way like my mother's husband, there to monitor her behavior and keep her in line.

Similarly, my mom's overprotectiveness wouldn't allow me to hold hands with the girls in kindergarten. I was told to walk home alone. As a teenager, I always felt guilty about going on a date, reluctant to bring them back to my poor neighborhood and my angry family, and when I got too close to a woman, I felt the need to run away.

At the time, I wasn't sure why, but thanks to my own counseling as an adult, I came to understand that I was attracted to women who were in need of help, as people I had to take care of and rescue…only to ultimately be repelled by their similarity to my mother. It took a while to learn to be attracted to women who were independent and psychologically stable.

Running, in fact, became a metaphor for my early life, and I was an accomplished sprinter in high school and college. But I couldn't truly run from my problems; there's no way to take off and leave your head behind, filled with all its bad imprinting.

But there are ways to get better.

As an adult, I got involved with my own counseling and came to recognize the source of my needing to evade intimacy.

In essence, I Chucked It! Can you ever entirely put your past behind you? Of course not! But you can learn to overcome the negative imprinting on your psyche, and you can learn to be stronger.

And for me, professionally, that pain from my childhood motivated me to want to make other people's lives and all of life's situations better. Whether it was my parents, my sister or later, with my professional associations and even people I'd encounter in daily life, I came to recognize that many other people have pain in their lives, just as I did, and I wanted to find a way to improve those circumstances.

I also came to understand that life should be fun and joyful. I felt it as a child at times, but it was always dampened by the negative and depressive perspective of my mother. She would say to me, "If you laugh in the morning, you'll cry at night," or "If you play music in the morning, something bad will happen if the afternoon." It's hard as a child to maintain an optimistic outlook, regardless of your personality, if such negativity is consistently poured over you.

There will always be negative people and negative situations. Chuck It! We either learn to ignore the negativity or we can succumb to it. Negativity is contagious, particularly when it's directed by parents, who by being our first emotional attachments in life have the power to inadvertently damage us, even when they might think they're teaching or protecting us. But negativity can follow us through life in many guises, and if we're ready to succumb to it, it will drag us down.

What's illuminating or unique about my childhood? Nothing, really. There are children who grow up in far worse environments. Some of them are forever dogged by that negative imprinting and never shake it. Others live cheerful, productive existences that don't betray the emotional privation of their childhood. Having a difficult childhood is not, by itself, ennobling or instructive. It's a poor start psychologically, but we all have the power to change that imprinting, to overcome the negativity and find purpose and joy in our lives, to Chuck the bad and embrace the good.

In my work, I often tell people that if they have no laughter, smiles and fun, they may end up being a supervisor! (Supervisors in life, who feel the pressure from those above them and the responsibility for those below them who endure the most stress; they're caught in a "supervisor sandwich.") To go through life without a sense of humor or sense of lightness, particularly when a part of you wants to feel those things, is tragic. And tragedy, we should always remember, is not mere sadness; it is sadness caused in spite of good intentions.

Most people have good intentions, but not everyone is capable of turning those intentions into healthy actions. (The road to hell, as they say, is paved with such good intentions.)

Everyone deserves to feel joy, and making the effort to correct flaws in our imprinting that prevent joy should be priority one. If only we cared for ourselves mentally and emotionally with the same diligence that we cared for our teeth. Laughter may or may not be the best medicine, but it certainly makes every situation more enjoyable, or at least more tolerable. Finding that joy in your life isn't selfish, or misspent time: it's essential.

And inspiration, as I came to realize, doesn't always come from a great role model. Sometimes, inspiration comes first from knowing what you don't want to do or be. Most of us have worked a job or had a relationship that illustrated to us precisely what we didn't want in life

I knew I didn't want to be like my parents, and I knew I didn't want to be trapped in Chelsea in the 1970s. Who would I be, and how would I overcome my unhappy early years?

Chapter Two
Finding Your Own Way

Patience

Every reading period
Robert would choose the book
The Little Train That Could
and
sit on my lap and listen
to the story.

He never stayed for the end,
but instead
would leave every time
at the same time.

It took six months
for Robert to remain
until the end of the book.

Now,
he brings books of different varieties
and smiles a lot.

The word "patience" has an interesting connotation: people tend to think of patience as waiting for something to happen. But patience isn't necessarily passive. In my life, patience played a large part, because good things aren't only hard to attain, they can also be tests of endurance...and patience.

Patience, rather than implying passivity, can mean actively pursuing a goal and not giving up when obstacles arise, or when the process feels like it's taking too long.

Don't mistake patience for doing nothing. Make patience an attribute, not a curse.

I never made the honor roll at Chelsea High School, and my SAT scores were average. Despite my average scholastic record, I had lofty ambitions. I was determined to make something extraordinary of my life.

I was a good athlete, I loved writing stories and poetry, and I loved nature, people and animals, and I was as girl-crazy as the next guy. I was always finding a stray dog to assist, a pigeon, or even an insect. I thought that one life was just as precious as another, and I couldn't bear to see anything harmed. My role as caretaker at home, the junior father who tried to keep things safe and sane, created in me a need to care for those who were in need.

And I had friends. I was captain of the track team and set a state sprinting record; I played baseball and basketball and seemed as normal as any other kid my age. I certainly didn't advertise the fear and depression that lurked beneath the surface. In those days, people didn't walk around with their hearts on their sleeves, and talking about your emotional issues wasn't fodder for daytime talk shows.

I worked summers as a playground instructor at Highland Park in Chelsea, and in a day camp that would take inner-city kids from Chelsea to a nice nature area in Essex, Massachusetts. When I was a head counselor, I tended to select junior counselors who were overweight and maybe a little rough around the edges. I wanted to mentor kids who were in need. I wanted to nurture people who needed a hand up.

Years later, when I was a gym teacher at a Montessori school at 99th Street and Broadway in New York City, I always wanted to share more of my time with the slower kids. I felt that the kids who could catch on more quickly would be fine…it was the slower kids who needed more assistance, and without the support of someone above them, they would even fall further behind.

I didn't consider myself an underdog, but I certainly identified with the kids who were underdogs. And there's a great deal of satisfaction in helping an underdog become if not a winner, a competitor. It elevates their self-esteem, and in doing so, it elevates our own. Anyone can back a winner.

I attended Bridgewater State College in Massachusetts as an undergraduate, majoring in English.

"I still remember Chuck sitting in my office," recalls Henry Fanning, who was dean of admissions at Bridgewater in those days. "You either like people right away or you don't, and there was something about his presence that I admired. I could see that he was very determined to succeed, and he was very honest about his lack of money and modest upbringing, but I could see that he was determined to push past that."

I enjoyed those years at Bridgewater, but I was also determined that, once I graduated that college, I wouldn't return there until I was invited back. And I was invited back, but that's a story for later in the narrative.

During the summer of my junior year in college, I met a young fellow who had just graduated from Tufts University. I had applied to Tufts, and was rejected there, as well as at Bates, Bowden, University of New Hampshire, University of Maine and several other colleges. A Massachusetts state college, Bridgewater had accepted me, and I was happy to go, living in a transient rooming house for eighty dollars a month. Anything was better than living in Chelsea with my family.

This Tufts graduate, Jim Kensellagh, told me I should think big and do more with my life. He said that I needed to extend myself, that I had potential to do great things. I thought so, too, but what twenty-year-old doesn't think he's capable of great things? I was happy just to be in college and away from home. But feeling free and being on your own isn't necessarily the same as pushing yourself to achieve, or reaching for the brass ring.

Don't get too complacent about your place in the universe. There's always something else to be achieved if you continually reset your sights.

Jim was going to graduate school at Columbia University in New York City, and he said he thought I should apply there, too. Just the thought of the hallowed halls of an Ivy League school thrilled me! Why not apply to a school that had always evoked such feelings in me? Why shouldn't I go to school there?

So I applied to Columbia, went to New York City for an interview, and to my amazement, I was accepted, and given a job to help me with my finances.

That opportunity was all I needed to be on my way.

My mom told me not to go, saying I would never make it, that I wasn't smart enough, but I had learned to not listen to the negativity. I wasn't yet in counseling, but I had learned to Chuck the voices that held me back. I knew I was ready for the challenge, and I knew I could make it.

This was a crucial juncture in my life, because if I had feared going to New York City, I wouldn't be where I am today, and if I had allowed the negativity to control me, I'd still be stuck in Chelsea, or at least in a Chelsea of the mind. I had decided, perhaps subconsciously more than consciously, that the negative things in my life would inspire me to do more, not less. I couldn't control what had happened to me; my entire life up to that point had been about not having control.

Chuck those feelings! Anything or anyone who fears your failure more than you do isn't protecting your feelings—they're protecting their own. And you owe yourself the option of adventure, even if that may lead to failure. Big things arise from big risks. All I was risking was my pride, and I was certain that if I worked hard enough, Columbia and New York City wouldn't overwhelm me.

I knew I could control how I responded to opportunities and challenges. I had resolved to make my life an adventure.

So I packed my bags and headed to New York City.

Chapter Three
Life in the City

Subway

Everyone is going somewhere.

*The homeless man
who sleeps
curled up in the corner.*

*The teenage boy
running away from his family
and riding all day.*

*People going to work;
some to meet their friends
and more.*

Everyone is going somewhere.

Going to Columbia was thrilling. Just the phrase "Ivy League" has a special connotation. I was going to attend an

Ivy League school in the world's most important city! Would I be up to the challenge? I wanted to find out. Bridgewater was a nice state school, and it had afforded me my first opportunity to be on my own and prove myself. But Columbia was special.

And then, despite having aspired to the goal of attending an Ivy League school from childhood, when I first got to New York City, I was overwhelmed.

First impression: New York is bigger and scarier than I expected.

It was all too much. The noise. The people. The ever-wakefulness of the city. I knew every pothole on Amsterdam Avenue, and I could tell, lying in bed in the middle of the night, which hole each passing truck had struck.

I came downtown, naively looking for a village in the middle of New York City. "Where is Greenwich Village?" I asked, as though there were some rustic and bucolic hamlet located in the middle of this teeming metropolis. "This *is* the Village," I was told.

Then I adjusted. Again, patience properly employed is a virtue. So is acceptance of the fact that there are things beyond our control or beyond our comprehension. It's okay not to have all the answers; it's okay to not have control all the time.

It's okay to be overwhelmed by things that are overwhelming, just like it's okay to laugh when something is funny, or to cry when you're sad. Natural emotions shouldn't have to fight their way to daylight.

It took some time, but gradually, I stopped fighting the vastness and noisiness of the city, and I began to embrace it. Like the negativity in my home that inspired me to move on, the vastness of New York City pushed me to excel. There would be no heroic rescues here any more than there had been any in my childhood; a city this big didn't care what my intentions were or whether I felt I was deserving or not: I would have to make my way on my own.

And there was justification for that persistent optimism. There were people from everywhere in the United States and all over the world in the city, and they were making it. From the Wall Street trader to the Lebanese guy selling falafel from a pushcart, each had come here to stake his or her claim, to find a niche. And if they could do it, so could I.

That's the magic of the human spirit: if you dare people to do something, or you tell them it's impossible, they'll go out and do it. We all have the capacity to be that dandelion that pushes up through the crack in the asphalt; it's just a matter of summoning the courage to do it.

New York City then became a revelation. It seemed everyone was going somewhere, physically and metaphorically. People here were as diverse as was humanly possible, yet I knew they were the same as the people in Chelsea, or Boston or Bridgewater. They were human beings with hopes and fears and aspirations, and they were all determined to make a way for themselves in the most exciting city in the world.

New York City no longer felt overwhelming. It felt like the nexus of civilization, and what could be more invigorating than living at the nexus of civilization?

Everywhere I looked, there was success: businesspeople, artists, musicians, actors, even the people selling from carts on the sidewalk. The opportunities to invent oneself anew, to find a niche and become successful on my own terms, seemed limitless. All it required was hard work and some sacrifice; there were people who had come from money here, of course, but the vast majority had little more going for them than their drive, perseverance and faith. As long as there were opportunities and money, people would come here, from the Korean grocers and Indian newspaper vendors to the Hungarian baker I bought bread from on Amsterdam Avenue.

None of these people had been born with a silver spoon in their mouth. Many had been born poorer than me, in countries that didn't afford opportunities like Ivy League educations, a thriving middle class and tolerance of diversity.

The energy and vitality of the city and its people inspired something deep within me. And when I accepted that limitless energy and learned to flow with it, I became a true resident, and a part of that energy.

I was studying psychology and education at Columbia, and I was working as a lifeguard and playground monitor to help earn my way, but I also learned a great deal about people just by walking around. There's no need to drive in New York City; you can walk or take public transportation everywhere. So I walked everywhere, and watched everyone: Europeans, Africans, Middle Easterners, transvestites, street musicians, homeless people.

New York City was a microcosm of the planet. I never felt lonely, even when I was on my own, because no matter when you walked about, there were people, and the visual and auditory stimulation of so many people was always there.

The sensibility that tells us unfamiliarity is scary? Chuck It! The notion that we can't compete as small fish in a big pond? Chuck It, too, until you've tried for yourself.

In a way, living in such a place helps you deal with your mortality a bit. There are so many people and so much going on around you that the life energy is almost ceaseless. Yes, we all die someday, but in this vast stew of humanity, each life is a part of some much larger continuum. Some people find so much humanity exhausting, but I found it invigorating.

My life was exciting in those days, but it was hardly balanced. I was so driven to succeed that I was perpetually in motion. I had yet to root out the negativity of my youth, and I denied myself intimacy in those days. Not that I was capable of intimacy; I had friends but few confidantes, and I still saw women as people I needed to protect, which eventually drove me away from them. My relationships tended to be short and intense, then quickly over. I equated intimacy with becoming a caregiver, and the last thing I had the time for was taking care of someone else, particularly someone I was subconsciously equating with my mother.

My friends tended to shrug off my behavior in relationships as being too picky, or wanting to be free of emotional ties. Actually, in the strongest way, I did want to connect with other people, but despite mustering up all the willpower I had, I couldn't seem to do it. I was connecting with people every day on levels that brought satisfaction to everyone's lives: there were friends, co-workers, even strangers who brought meaning to my life. But not intimacy.

I didn't understand why I behaved the way I did, but that insight was coming, as were many other opportunities and revelations.

Chapter Four
Changing Your Path

Hello

*Looking at myself
in the mirror
at the barber shop,
I wonder if that's me.*

*I say hello
to myself
to make sure.*

I made something of myself in the city.

I graduated from Columbia with two master's degrees and all my doctoral credits and got a position at St. John's Hospital in Far Rockaway, Queens, working in a field that was relatively new at the time: patient counseling. It involved counseling and play and recreational therapy with sick children and their families. I took the A train from Manhattan an hour and a half to Far Rockaway, worked with my patients, took the train back, and often worked a part-time job as well.

I wasn't making a lot of money, but I had lived frugally my entire life, so it didn't bother me. Growing up, we'd never had any money, and going to college, I'd never had any money. But my aspirations didn't have anything to do with accumulating things or living in style; some people compensate for an impoverished childhood by acquiring things, but not me.

My work was very fulfilling, but I took similar jobs much closer to home when the opportunities arose, securing positions at Beth Israel Hospital and the Hospital for Joint Diseases, both located on 17th Street in Manhattan. I could walk or take the bus to work now.

But at all three hospitals, there was a sense that the work I was doing was administratively hard to justify. Even though the ostensible goal of a hospital is patient care, it's also a business, and the functions that generate the most revenue are given higher priority and more power. In every hospital, surgeons are the kings. Counseling wasn't generating much revenue, and my salary reflected this lack of enthusiasm for a "nonessential" service.

Of course, what I was doing was essential. But I knew that no matter how good I was at my job, no matter how many people I genuinely helped, I would never fit into the power cliques that exerted so much influence in the hospital. And I wanted to help people, but not with my hands tied behind my back. Is it really a service if it's done begrudgingly by the hospital, and falls short of the care people actually need?

Then there was the administrative issue. I soon realized that I spent more time in meetings, talking about patient care or not talking about patient care, than I spent actually caring for patients. Like any other large organization, hospitals have so many administrative layers, so many layers of management and communication channels, that eventually, the boat is too big to steer.

It was a lesson in business for someone with no business acumen: too many decision-makers actually prevent decisions from being made, and too many chiefs guarantee there won't be enough warriors to get the actual work done.

And every organization, I learned, is governed as much by insider politics as it is by sound, practical business decisions. And a service that comes to be viewed primarily as a revenue stream is at odds with its purpose. Patient counseling is an intangible asset with real benefits, but identifying it only by its bottom-line value equates it with tangible products, like a toaster or a soda. Surgery is evaluated the same way, but at least there's a tangible outcome to evaluate. Yes, the appendix has been removed and the fever has subsided.

How do you know someone with serious mental or emotional problems has been fixed?

One day, I realized that my walk to work had gradually grown longer. It had been thirty minutes, then thirty-five, then forty… I was taking longer to get there as my frustration increased. Worse, no one seemed to care what time I arrived.

So I began asking myself: is this what I want to do with my life? And if not, what *do* I want to do with my life?

I had been taking a course on employee assistance programs (EAP), which in those days largely consisted of substance abuse counseling. And I started thinking: what if this concept of employee assistance was expanded beyond substance abuse? What if employee assistance included counseling on family dynamics, work stress, depression, children's issues? What if employee assistance was more broadly defined as any counseling issue that assisted the employee and his or her family?

I hadn't invented anything new with this line of thought—just proposed an expansion of an existing service. But suddenly, I felt like I had discovered something that no one had thought of yet.

Why limit the counseling services we're offering people? Open the gates to every serious issue people have!

Around the same time I had my revelation, an issue arose at work that presented me with an opportunity to leave the hospitals. Should I take this as a sign to leave my existing jobs and run with my expanded EAP idea? The notion was irresistible.

The notion wasn't irresistible to my family and friends, of course. My parents, having endured the Depression and being cautious about life in general, were appalled by my impulse. Their formula was, you get out of school (if you're lucky enough to go to school), you find a good job and you cling to it until you retire. "You have no business experience, New York is a tough city, it'll never work, get a job teaching if you don't want to work in a hospital, move back to the Boston area... With all the people who go into business every year, what makes you think you can do it?" These were some of the comments from my friends and family. But I didn't blame them for being cautious; that was what they believed, and what they thought was best for me.

So I Chucked my career, and started over in uncharted territory. I quit my job and went into business for myself.

I wasn't deterred. I knew inside myself that I was capable of doing whatever I set my mind to doing.

Chapter Five
Being Bold

Fire

*Your life is recorded
on a card
the size of a matchbook.*

*You think,
something must be missing.*

*Soon,
even the matchbook
will be gone.*

Boldness: it's a quality we associate with heroes and leaders but often, we don't see the difference between being bold and being foolish. Sometimes that difference is only apparent in retrospect, but life can't be lived in retrospect. So, being bold requires taking risks based on informed choices rather than purely on instincts.

My instincts about the expanded EAP program I wanted to sell were *right*, but making a correct assumption is only step one. We all have instincts that are correct: I can go to graduate school; I do have the ability to make it as an actor; I am smart enough to do this job. Many people give instinct short shrift. (The phrase "women's intuition," for example, is usually used derisively, but there's value in those intuitive thoughts.)

But intuition isn't enough.

Step two in this process is creating a plan for success and implementing it. That means researching your endeavor before blindly attempting it. Let's say being an actor is your intuitive ability. Don't simply hop on a bus and head to New York or Los Angeles. That's why both cities are overwhelmingly populated by frustrated waiters, cabbies and porn performers. Take acting lessons, go on auditions, get professionally evaluated. Don't assume that your ability will shine through a lack of experience or preparation. Everyone likes "overnight success" stories, but they're extremely rare. That's what makes them so exciting—they almost never happen in real life.

Step three is tenacity—a refusal to give up or give in once you've committed to your bold move.

I know that not everyone is a big risk taker, but taking calculated risks needn't require changes as dramatic as quitting your job and creating a service that no one yet knows they want, or going to college in New York and living on a shoestring. It could be steps as simple as talking to someone you'd like to meet, trying food you're unfamiliar with or traveling somewhere you've never been before. Better to live life making the occasional misstep than spend your years regretting the chances that weren't taken and the opportunities that were missed, and bold moves needn't make headlines to be personal triumphs.

In making my bold decision, I had some safety nets in place. I still had my master's degree in psychology and education, so becoming a therapist or teacher, or some similar career path, was still an option for me. I had also continued to work second jobs even when I was working at two hospitals; I was continually teaching or coaching on the side, mostly because I loved working with kids, and because I was perpetually in motion. At this point in my life, I was still running from my past, and no down time meant no time to reflect on the pain I was still struggling to understand. But, at least I used my propensity for perpetual motion productively.

I also had a luxury-free life. I lived in a small apartment with my cat, and had roughly twenty-seven different recipes involving tuna. I was very frugal, having lived that way my entire life, so my overhead was minimal. If anyone could take a chance on a new business without great risk, it was someone in my economic position.

Some people are reluctant to take a risk because it might mean giving up the comforts to which they're accustomed. Few of us aspire to live with progressively fewer niceties as we grow older. But making a bold move may require giving up the luxuries we come to see as necessities.

Chuck It! Objects come and go, and money is only as valuable as what you use it for. Boldness requires seeing beyond going to the movies on Friday night or buying the latest technological gizmo, and making the occasional sacrifice.

I was determined to succeed. I felt I had made a discovery, a service that was both original and needed. I'm no genius, but I could see the potential for what I wanted to do, and I was blessed with an inborn bullshit detector. Good common sense is sometimes more valuable than book smarts, and I knew the writing was on the wall in hospital care. (That medical care in this country has since become even more obsessed with the bottom line is tragic, and will be the subject of later chapters.) While the work I was doing was beneficial to my patients and to me personally, it was of secondary importance to the administrators. Hospital care was a commodity weighed by dollars and cents, and putting extra money into an intangible service like counseling didn't enhance the business' bottom line.

I made a brochure offering my expanded EAP services and mailed it to businesses in the tri-state area. I was wary of soliciting businesses close to where I lived in Greenwich Village, because I had no office—just my two-hundred-square-foot studio, a fourth-floor walk-up apartment. I was more comfortable with the notion of calling on prospective customers than with them coming to see me.

I had no business training, just the informed notion that I had something beneficial to offer and a determination to succeed.

The next nine months would test that belief.

Chapter Six
Making Some Sacrifices

World

For all your pain
I still love you.

Some flowers bloom
only in water,
others in the dry land of desert;
yet they are all flowers.

We stand miles from each other
and I cry for the possibilities
of this life.

And still
I love you.

People have a lot of ego about their work, and for many, it's the best representation of who they are. *See? I'm a great salesman... My decisions saved the company millions... I keep people out of jail...*

While we all have our "dream" job (which is actually very possibly your worst nightmare), no job is beneath you if it serves your needs. My needs were twofold: have an income while I tried to get my new business off the ground, and find satisfaction. Fortunately, any job where I interacted with people and felt I was helping them gave me satisfaction.

So I worked for Snap-A-Grad, taking photographs at graduations, sometimes shooting thousands of pictures of smiling graduates receiving their diplomas. I changed diapers—I became quite the authority on cloth versus disposable—at Tiny House Nursery School in the Village. I was a gym teacher at a school on 99th Street. I worked as an adjunct at Bloomfield College in Brooklyn, teaching psychology, English, education—basically anything they needed taught. And I was the head coach of men's and women's track and field and women's volleyball at Pratt Institute in Brooklyn.

I had always preferred noncompetitive athletics, even though I'd been a very good competitive runner. As a coach, I just wanted everyone to have fun and get some exercise. The program at Pratt was very small, even for a Division III art and architecture college. I think we lost every volleyball match that season, but we had a lot of fun.

For one match, we had to drive to Marymount in upper Manhattan, and I got lost. (I was also the bus driver; we were *that* small.) The opposing coach was gung-ho, so I asked her to take it easy on us, knowing we were going to lose no matter what. She had *no* sense of humor, and they demolished us, but afterwards, we went out for pizza and laughed it off.

Meanwhile, I was calling every business I thought could use my program in the hope of selling the idea. Businesspeople would schedule appointments and hear my pitch, but ultimately, no one was interested. I was getting a sense that people thought the EAP was a good idea, but it hadn't yet reached a point where most employers saw it as *essential*.

I was rejected by eighty businesses. That's a lot of rejection. Mail rejections are one thing, and being ignored can be discouraging, but I was putting on a suit and traveling by bus or train or plane to an appointment, briefcase in hand, and making an earnest pitch, only to be rejected. It was a whole other level of disappointment.

And selling it in person was essential, I realized. It was the only way to properly convey the level of integrity and service I intended to provide. There's no substitute for face time and human contact. Shaking hands, hugging, speaking face to face and making eye contact were integral to what I was proposing. I was the man who would help their employees; the trust they needed to have in me as a person was an implicit part of the package.

One time, I had two prospective clients, representatives from Barclay's Bank and Lloyd's Bank, and I took them to lunch at Arthur's Tavern. When the bill came and I had to pay two hundred dollars that I really didn't have, I was stunned. *I don't know how I'm going to keep doing this*, I thought.

Some nights, I'd lie in bed and look at my clock. It would be three o'clock a.m., and I had to start calling people again in the morning, and they'd be telling me they weren't interested, or hanging up. But I didn't quit.

I had only one phone. I couldn't afford to buy a fax machine, so when I had to fax, I would run across the street and send it from the neighborhood deli.

I persevered, truly believing in my mission and knowing that I had the monetary and emotional resources to keep going. I'd learned that as a marathon runner. I would "hit the wall," as runners often say, around mile twenty, feeling fatigued and dizzy and short of breath and dead tired. But if I pushed past it, I'd get what runners call "second wind," the reserve of energy required to cross the finish line. I needed a second wind.

I had friends who had also been bold, thought big and ventured out on their own. And they had hit the wall and pulled off, never to finish the race. I knew better. I was confident in my idea and my ability to deliver it. It wasn't a matter of *if*; it was a matter of *when*.

I clearly remember looking back at my cat, perched in the window five floors above me, and saying out loud, "Kitty, I'm going out there and making a sale today." I had no one else to say that to, but I was The Little Train That Could, and the boy who I read it to every day in daycare. After countless times of trying to get through that book and becoming frustrated and losing interest, we finished the book and moved on. That small act of persistence had seemed to soothe and encourage him.

I would not be distracted from my task.

Finally, I had a small job request, and I dug into that. It wasn't enough to pay the bills, but it was my first opportunity to try out my theories. It was great getting my feet wet, but I had yet to hit my stride.

And then I made an appointment to visit the Golden Nugget in Atlantic City.

Chapter Seven
Meeting a Need

Love Poem

Where do you love
if it is not here?

Future never arrives.
Past is to remember
and
learn from.

So,
where do you love
if it is not here?

Your nature is everywhere.

The small job request I got was from a bank in New York City, Credit Lyonnais, which was laying off an employee and needed someone to assist with his outplacement. Such an assignment probably seems like a small place to start, particularly with my vision of expanding employee assistance programs in every imaginable way, but to this employee it wasn't a small job, and it was my only job. I knew that doing right by this man and providing the service I had promised was important for everyone involved.

No job is so small that it shouldn't be done right, and everyone's problems are important to themselves. Businesspeople should have that ethos etched into their souls if they intend to provide a service that truly benefits their customers and clients.

To this day, in my business, I try to provide every client with as much attention as I am able to personally provide for that one man.

Even with one man, it was a good opportunity to apply the extended employee assistance program I had been envisioning. This man, having been dismissed but still in need of assistance, had been placed alone in a windowless room, with only a pad of paper and a phone. It was the closet thing to solitary confinement I had ever seen in a business.

I was embarrassed for him, and he was embarrassed as well, but I knew it was my job to make him feel empowered despite the uncomfortable circumstances. I knew as I worked with him that I enjoyed making him feel good about himself, that he was important, and that he could make a difference somewhere. He had been sentenced to this confinement, but he needed to know that he hadn't been forgotten by the world. I was part therapist, part motivator, part instructor and part coach.

I provided him with leads from the newspaper, helped him write letters, developed his resume and provided coaching until he got another job. I loved the experience, and we both benefited from working together. He benefited by finding a new job and a renewed sense of his worth.

And I proved that I could do what I thought I could do, at least on a small scale. The instinct that my expanded EAP services could work was correct. The initial experience had confirmed that. Now all I needed was a chance to provide those services on a grand scale.

It was during this initial experience that I received a call from the Golden Nugget in Atlantic City.

The Golden Nugget was owned by Steve Wynn, the casino developer who reinvented the industry in Las Vegas and is known for his vision, his business acumen and his insistence on excellence. I was going to have to find a way to impress anyone who worked for Steve Wynn.

This would be a challenge.

I didn't have a car, which probably sounds implausible to outsiders but perfectly logical to people who live in Manhattan. So I went to the Port Authority and took a Lucky Streak Bus to Atlantic City. It was summer, unfortunately, because I only owned one suit, and it was made of wool. Thinking pragmatically, I'd bought it thinking it would be of use in every season, but wool in summer is an unforgiving fabric.

I arrived in Atlantic City and went dripping with sweat into my appointment with Paula Rowland and Arte Nathan, who were running the Golden Nugget's personnel department. (This is before they were called "human resources departments.") I was excited by the opportunity, but after appraising my disheveled appearance, Arte began telling me why I had wasted their time by scheduling the appointment.

"He was more than disheveled," says Paula Rowland, recalling the meeting. "He was a mess, but he was completely unpretentious and very earnest."

"We have some of the biggest companies in the United States—Blue Cross Magellan, Aetna—trying to get our business," Arte said after appraising my appearance. "How are you going to compete with that?"

"I have to admit, this is my first day in Atlantic City and my first time in a casino, but if you want a program that works, give me the opportunity," I challenged them. "Put me to work here in the casino, and I'll show you what I can do."

I had nothing to lose by being honest. And being a one-man operation, I was in no position to dazzle them with glorious promises of what I could do. All I could do was be honest.

Not everyone appreciates honesty, and some people will make safe choices or fall prey to overblown promises. When you're the little guy, the upstart, all you can promise is that you know your strengths and that you're committed to working hard and providing the needed service or product. If you're genuine, there are people who will recognize that.

The notion that you have to gild the lily by exaggerating your abilities or background, or by making promises you know you can't keep? Chuck It! The business world is full beyond its quota of such people, which is why so many companies suffer with poor public perceptions of them.

Honesty isn't the *best* policy; it's the *only* policy.

And Arte and Paula liked my honesty, and recognized my sincerity. They also knew that the sales and marketing people who were so anxious to sell Golden Nugget their services would disappear once the deal was made, and they'd never see them again. They'd dealt with the "professional" salespeople before, and knew their rap by heart. I promised to be hands-on, beginning to end, and to work hard. It was all I could promise.

So Arte and Paula Chucked It, forgoing the safe choice that many executives would have made, and took on The Little Train That Could. Because I made them believe I could, and I immediately backed up that promise and rewarded their faith.

"It's a lesson in not judging books by their covers," says Paula. "Luckily for me and luckily for the employees of the Golden Nugget, we made the right choice."

I couldn't work in the pit with the dealers and pit bosses because I would've needed a special license, but I did virtually every other job. I was as hands-on as was permissible. I was a bus greeter, helping the senior citizens on and off the bus, looking bright-eyed when they arrived and foggy when they left; I worked it the restaurants and talked to the cocktail waitresses, who were weighed every week to ensure they maintained their ideal weight, including some who had eating disorders and substance abuse issues; I walked the casino floor around the clock and learned about the lives of the dealers and pit bosses, and even the maintenance people.

I talked to the union reps and members and I talked to management. I talked to employees not only about what their jobs were like, but what their lives were like away from work. People are the same all over, but different careers create different problems, and I didn't want a one-size-fits-all solution for an industry that was unique, and I wanted people at literally every position in that casino to have access to help that would be tailored to them.

It was an expansive approach to a healthcare industry program that had been a one-size-fits-all Band-aid. It was bold, it took a lot of time and care, and when I was done, I had created the first comprehensive employee assistance program for a casino.

"We had around thirty-seven hundred employees, and for many of them it was their first good-paying job, and some of them were reckless with the freedom that money brought," recalls Paula. "There were issues with drugs and alcohol, with gambling and infidelity, and Chuck was can-do about everything. All he'd lacked was the proper platform to showcase what he could do, and he was able to build one of the most successful programs in Atlantic City."

That program I created has since become the model for all hotel and casino EAPs worldwide.

"Chuck was completely qualified and creative in his approach," says Paula. "But I still tease him about eating his salad that day with his fingers. And I'm pretty sure he still has that sweaty brown-wool suit."

I admit, I didn't have the polish of my competitors, but I had the *approach* they wanted.

And they took a chance on me, and I repaid their confidence.

The next question, of course, was: could I develop programs like that for every company I worked with?

Why not? In creating customized EAPs for employers, I was ahead of what the rest of the industry was doing. I continue to this day to create custom programs. I remain ahead of that curve because the healthcare industry has finally learned that it has to provide *more* services for employees, though they still aren't committed to providing *better* services. (*What's the bottom line?* is their mantra, as though human psyches are automobiles or paper cups. *How do we do this and make money, and where can we cut corners to make it more profitable?*)

I had a different bottom line: how do I make my company the best it can possibly be so that it meets the needs of everyone with access to it? And, not incidentally, how do I become the best person I can possibly be in the meantime?

Chapter Eight
Persevere...

Morning

Slowly walking in the morning,
with the sun moving
from behind the clouds and
gently warming the air.

I smile a joyful tear
for this day.

I like the word "persevere." "Per" reminds me of "persistence" and the idea of charging onward even when the going is difficult. "Severe" reminds me that the obstacles can be very tough.

I wasn't content with my success with the Golden Nugget. I was providing EAP to everyone who needed it there, but there were so many other people who could use the service. I truly wanted to develop a business that made a difference in the world. That probably sounds like an idealistic statement from someone who has actually succeeded in business, but it's true, and I didn't have this revelation only after I had conquered my competitors and been besieged by guilt. I firmly believed it all along, and I continue to believe that we can improve the world with our actions.

I bet my career on it, and I was right.

Not that I was entirely altruistic. I wanted my business to succeed, as all businesspeople do. (Individual people can be entirely altruistic, but no business can afford to follow a model that *never* puts the interests of the business first.) But my business, unlike most, was committed to hinging its success on the improved well-being of others.

The expanded EAP idea was hatched from a place within me that has always believed that it's important to help those with problems, as individuals and as a society. Everyone has difficulties, some more obvious and extreme than others, and the better suited each individual is to support himself and support others, the healthier society is in general. I wanted a business that could be a mentor for people, and I wanted to mentor those I encountered.

And of course, I wanted to grow my company. There's no point in making a bold decision and creating a beneficial service if you're not committed to making that service available to everyone who needs it.

Obviously, I couldn't meet the counseling or crisis needs of Golden Nugget employees by myself, so I contracted psychologists and licensed therapists in every necessary field to provide individualized counseling for everyone who called the numbers I established. And I set to ensuring that the people who answered those phones, the very first people who came into contact with those in need, were psychologists with experience in counseling.

Let me repeat that: the people who answer my phones have at least a master's degree in psychology.

That may sound like an obvious personnel decision, but it's actually the opposite of the norm in the EAP industry. At the large healthcare companies, this initial contact (called "triage," just as it's called in an emergency room or on a battlefield) is handled by…well, people trained in how to answer the phone. Why should it be any other way? The large healthcare companies handle your medical health questions in the same manner. Do you believe your mental well-being is any more of a priority to them than your physical health?

The triage I established was in my new apartment on 42nd Street in Manhattan, which in those days wasn't the family-friendly area it is today. I had six hundred square feet to work in, and that's all I did there: work. Again, I was accustomed to living a rather Spartan existence, so it didn't trouble me that the space was filled with office furniture, and that there was no bed. I needed room for my employees.

I hired several people to work triage answering phones, and I answered phones myself. Day and night, every day and night, for years. And it was the casino industry, in which people are working round the clock. There are no off days and there is no down time. And since I couldn't rightly ask my employees to work all night and on weekends, much of that responsibility fell to me. And why not? It was my business model, and I had finally implemented it. Who better to man the phones?

My personal life, rather than suffering, was virtually non-existent. Sometimes during the day, I'd curl up by the fireplace and nap for a few hours while people worked around me. I had no bed, after all, and I literally lived at the office. Where else could I sleep?

I was running again, of course; I'd run track to escape, I'd run to New York City and now I was running a business full-time. Part of that running was because I was completely committed to doing something I believed in, of course, but

I could have made time for myself if I truly wanted it. But I was still suffocated by intimacy. And yes, I vaguely sensed that I wasn't a fully functioning human being living in this way, but I was too busy to analyze it, so I didn't address it.

There were opportunities to address my workaholic lifestyle, to Chuck It, but I wasn't ready yet. And as with any self-improvement, there can be no remedy until the patient is wholly willing.

Eventually, I would understand that in order to heal, we must identify our problems, identify the remedies, and then aggressively engage them, just as we would a medical problem. Again, the subconscious mind is as much our constant companion as our body. We should treat it with the same attention to wellness.

So I continued to seek out clients. On Valentine's Day I visited Campbell Soup in Camden, New Jersey. At this point, I had fully established my EAP program at the Golden Nugget, and I knew the best way I could emphasize the value of what I provided was by showing the Campbell representative how my program worked in actuality, not just in theory.

So I brought Campbell's director in charge of developing the company's EAP program to Atlantic City to see the people at the Golden Nugget and let them speak for the program.

I could see on his face that he was impressed by the scope of the supervisory training, the twenty-four/seven service, and the knowledge I had of the gaming industry. The strategy worked: the executives and employees at the Golden Nugget sold him on my services.

"What can you do for me in Downingtown?" he asked. Campbell owned a big Pepperidge Farm plant in Downingtown, Pennsylvania.

"Leave it to me and I'll make it happen," I promised.

"I'd like to meet your staff this Thursday," he said.

"We'll be there," I promised.

I had never been to Downingtown, Pennsylvania. Plus, I thought he'd said Downeytown, so I didn't even have the proper name of the town when I set out to find it. The next morning, I took Amtrak to Downingtown (I didn't own a car), then switched to the Septa line, and by that afternoon, I had my staff and was ready for our meeting.

The next day, we met in Downingtown. He talked with my staff, and he was ready to sign the contract. And my business grew yet again, much to my satisfaction.

The obvious lesson here is perseverance, but there is a more subtle message here: happy customers are your best advertising. It's oft-quoted (and possibly apocryphal) that happy customers tell a friend, but unhappy ones tell five. Your best pitch should be live testimony, not a theoretical of what you "could do." "Could do" is a loaded phrase, because people don't live in potentials, they live in reality, and what you've actually done is far better evidence of your ability and your conviction than any "could do" you can muster.

And if the examples are lacking, and all you're holding are "could dos," it may be time to analyze your way of doing business, and Chuck It if it's not gaining you any ground.

Our everyday interactions with people are no different. Don't make empty promises, telling people what you could do for them; actions speak louder than words. Do what you say you'll do, and don't promise what you can't deliver.

Personal relationships, just like customers and clients, can be lost over empty promises.

Chapter Nine
...and Break Through

Wisdom

There's a type of
carelessness
with children
and old people.

An innocence that comes
from not knowing
or forgetting
what to know.

How do we measure success?

Most people will tell you that success is defined by intangibles, like their friends and family and the balance in their life. Few people admit that they keep score by acquiring things, whether it's the big house, the sports car or the trophy wife. But clearly those people exist, and while we may pity (or secretly envy) them, each of us has an internal meter with which we measure whether we've "made it."

Defining whether your business is a success is no easier.

You can follow the rapacious corporate raider prototype who acquires companies so he or she can downsize them or export their services or sell them off piecemeal. Need I say that acquisition for its own sake is empty? That premise isn't entirely obvious to some people, as the rise and fall of dozens of such companies has been thoroughly documented in recent years.

And how do you measure success when there's another company to acquire around the corner?

Now, substitute words like "woman" or "sports car" or "country club" for "company," and you can see how this business prototype is personified in some folks' personal lives.

Such behavior is empty of meaning and damaging to the psyche of all involved. So Chuck It!

My business was growing, but I hadn't reached the level of success I wanted. There are advantages to growing slowly, because I was still capable of handling each account personally, even though I had to assign most of the actual counseling to others. (To this day, I still spend a quarter of my work time answering the phones, doing triage work, because I still enjoy the opportunity to personally help people.) I didn't assign the personal attention—my version of "salesmanship"—to someone else, either. I still wanted to personally meet with management and employees, learn on-the-job about their businesses and their lives and assure them that we would provide them with what they needed.

I had a client, Schwan's, which operated a food delivery business, so I offered to accompany one of the drivers on his route. The day I scheduled to work the route, there was a torrential rainstorm in Chicago. I was heading to their headquarters in my rental car when I made a wrong turn and drove into a river.

Chuck It

I got out of the car safely, albeit soaking wet, carrying nothing but my gym bag. The last thing I saw was the top of the car floating down the river.

I walked through backyards and down side streets to find my way to the meeting. When I made my presentation to their board of directors, I started to tell them the story of my damp arrival.

"Did you see that car floating down the river?" someone asked.

"That was mine," I answered.

The story gave them evidence of my dedication, and by extension the dedication of my company, to providing the best service possible: I had come to Chicago to ride along with a driver, I had ditched a car in a river during a rain storm but still made my scheduled meeting, and still intended to learn their business from the ground up, even though it was still pouring rain.

Such stories make an indelible impression on prospective clients.

Then I went to the depot to ride along with a delivery truck. That was work! We were in and out of the truck more than two hundred times that day, and the day lasted twelve hours. My back ached and my legs hurt, and I was dog-tired by the time I got to bed that night.

So what's unique about a food delivery business? I discovered that many people who use such a service are elderly or disabled, or virtual shut-ins; many have no one to keep them company, and they want to have someone to talk to. The delivery people become more than just delivery people—they become listeners and storytellers, and they hear the gamut of human experiences: marriages, divorces, birthdays, grief and loneliness issues. The regular delivery person, in essence, becomes more than just a delivery person: he or she becomes a friend of the family.

Most people don't have training as therapists, but we all have ears, and that's all most people want when they talk: receptive ears and a sympathetic voice. We're all capable of being that person, and even in triage, where we're taking calls from people with severe psychological issues, personal crises and substance abuse issues, a portion of the callers simply want someone to talk to, someone to listen empathetically, and we do that, too.

And, in turn, those who listen, both professionally and as empathetic human beings, need to be able to tell their stories as well. And so the cycle of compassion is potentially infinite, if we all take the time to listen to each other.

So we customized the support for the Schwan's employees, providing them with psychological, financial and family support services, and just providing their employees someone to talk to.

At each client, I would walk the plant or visit as many locations as I was allowed, both so I could understand the specifics of the industry I was servicing and so people could talk to me and better understand about the service. It's important to demystify the counseling experience, because employees who understand the process and aren't intimidated by it are more likely to use it.

I flew out to the Unilever Best Foods plant in San Francisco, on Bryant Street, when they were a new client, where plant manager George Bleffert introduced me to all the employees.

"I know the names and family names of everyone here," he said. He told me that a good supervisor needs to be where the people are so he can listen to their issues and needs. That's where the real action in a company is—with the people who work there. "They become part of your family," he said.

George and I visited every aspect of the business, from

marketing to sales to manufacturing to reception to janitorial, and on every shift.

It was reinforced in me then, as it's been reinforced many times since: if you want to be successful you need to be there with the people who make the business run. It also drove home a perspective that I still embrace: it's a blessing to start small and grow gradually. You can deliver services better for clients if your service is personal, and growth is gradual.

And it's important to me to stay small enough to continue that kind of personal service. I don't need to own the largest EAP provider in the world. (Though we are currently the eighth largest in the United States, and the only one in the top ten that's privately owned.) I want to run the *best* EAP provider in the world.

By now, I was several years into my EAP creation, and I was, by most people's standards, a success. I had a thriving business, I was providing needed services to people, and my business was continuing to grow, but not so fast that I couldn't be "hands-on" with each of my clients and employees.

My days were full, my goals had been achieved to a certain degree, but there was still something missing. And I was still running from my responsibility to myself to fix the problem.

All that bad psychological imprinting and emotional baggage I had carried since childhood? It was time to Chuck It! And, as someone who provided professional counseling, it was time I recognized that I needed to get some for myself.

The next step to my success wasn't another transaction, or a supermodel or a sports car: it was good mental health. And that goal, just like success, would be hard to measure.

But just having it as a goal was a good place to start.

Chapter 10
Improving Self-Esteem

Child's Story

Is our education so immense
that we forget the beauty
of a hairline,
of a pencil mark,
some glue or some ink?

A child's teacher reads a story,
and turns the page quickly
without
stopping to pause.
Mental image is missed,
as guide hurries for the next word.

So many poems lost.
So many minds tossed
hurrying
for the next word.

Psychologically healthy people have good self-esteem, but it's important to properly define self-esteem. Healthy self-esteem comes from acceptance of one's self—not in the sense that all our problems are beyond our control or a resignation that we are damaged and unworthy of praise, but in finding a comfort with who we are as people, a feeling that we deserve love and positive attention, and that our lives have meaning and there is mutual benefit in our relationships with others.

Good self-esteem also shouldn't be confused with narcissism, a self-love that denies the feelings of others when they inconvenience one's self. People with good self-esteem don't wreak havoc in the emotional lives of others; part of healthy self-esteem is the recognition that the self-esteem of others is valuable as well.

How much self-esteem we have as individuals is a good measure of our culture, because there's huge disparity between the haves and the have-nots. But in our society, there's no reason we can't all become haves in the self-esteem department.

My self-esteem issues put up red flags all around me, but I was too busy to notice them, and too afraid to confront them when I did glimpse them. Step one with any issue is identifying the problem, and once I stopped running and realized that I wanted to be able to enjoy fulfilling relationships and that I deserved time to relax and the relish the rewards of my success, I was able to go to a therapist and talk about my childhood and the negative feelings those years had embedded in me, feelings that affected every relationship I'd had since.

I had always been embarrassed to tell anyone about the turmoil inside me. I certainly didn't confide it to my friends or my girlfriends. In the strongest way, I did want to connect, and yet I seemed incapable despite mustering all the willpower I had to do it. Ironically, my own pain had led me to the realization that other people must be going through their own type of pain, and into the field of psychology, and from there into a career where I could assist not just individuals but potentially, thousands of people. I was able to help all these other people to uncover their pain and issues and place them on the path of living a healthy life.

Could I now do the same thing for myself?

This is a huge Chuck It, the hardest thing any of us will ever have to do: ask for help with our psychological issues. It's still a vigorous discarding of what's wrong in our lives, but letting go, the actual act of parting with that bad early imprinting, isn't easy. For some people, it's a daily battle, no different than alcoholism or drug addiction: we are never *done* with it, we are never completely *healed*, but with counseling we are aware, we are self-correcting, and we are unburdened.

We are all, after all, works in progress.

Our reflexive response to psychic pain is to push things under the rug. Sometimes this avoidance even works for a while, but eventually, that pile gets bigger, the rug gets lumpier and harder to negotiate, and we trip over it in the form of depression, unhealthy or abusive relationships, and substance abuse to mask the pain. I knew from my clinical experience and the hundreds of people that I had counseled that it wouldn't just go away on its own, because it never goes away. Who we are is who we are.

But with the proper counseling, support and coaching, over time, I could be more aware of what was going in my head, and gradually I could develop new habits and not fall into familiar, unhealthy habits. And, I knew that I couldn't beat on myself if I occasionally slipped into those familiar, unhealthy behaviors.

Work in progress, work in progress…

One thing I had to learn was how to trust my instincts. Most of us have an intuitive sense of what feels right and what feels wrong psychologically, but those instincts can be marred by our early imprinting. My instinctive response to many people is to like them, but my next impulse, created by my years of being the caretaker in my family, is to try to protect them. Being the perpetual parent creates conflicts in any relationship (including parent-child!), and it can be the death of intimacy.

I had to learn to let go. This meant not feeling that I had to take care of everyone, trusting my instincts in my relationships, allowing things to happen without fretting over my lack of control, and learning to *enjoy* my life.

I had to learn how to be selfish.

We all know people we consider to be selfish, and they're not fun to be around. No one but the narcissist enjoys the narcissist's company. But for a compassionate person, finding occasion for being selfish merely means finding some joy in life and making decisions that truly benefit you. Being a caretaker isn't selfish, though some of the behaviors may seem selfish, because the caretaker is actually making *himself* happy. (Nor is he necessarily making those he's caring for happy by controlling every aspect of *their* lives.) It's similar to the person who believes he or she is being selfish by behaving in self-destructive ways, indulging themselves with women or sex or expensive toys, which never bring actual happiness.

Proper selfishness is hard to achieve. And those capable of acting in their own self-interest—behaving selfishly—typically make those around them happier as well.

I had to learn to enjoy life, so my counselor had me bring home funny movies. "When you hear people laughing, you'll laugh too," he told me.

I tried, but I didn't get the desired effect. "I didn't think they were funny," I explained.

"Fake it," he said. "When you hear people laugh, you'll laugh too, and if you don't learn to laugh, you'll end up like those supervisors."

This comment *did* make me laugh. But once I understood why my brain was the way it was, I was able to identify those moments when my bad imprinting would respond to a situation and override my instinct. And, with that ability and continued, I was on my way to better mental health.

Chapter Eleven
The Self-Esteem Gap

Beautiful Poem

I want to draw
you
into this poem.
It is
as beautiful
as you.

At the heart of most EAP issues is self-esteem. It's difficult to treat yourself well, to behave selfishly, when you don't feel well psychologically. Substance abuse, depression, obsessive-compulsive disorder…you name it, and the root cause is low self-esteem.

Where do these self-esteem problems come from? The basis for our self-esteem is formed when we're young. Ideally, we all have parents who love and care for each other, and for us and our siblings, and everyone is made to feel secure. We all grow up feeling like the world is safe and things will somehow be okay.

Most of us did not grow up in that *Ozzie and Harriet* or *Cosby Show* type of household. (Choose your ideal based on your generation, but television's persistent need to show perfect families that exist *only* on television has created fifty years of children wondering why no one they know looks or acts like the people who are being broadcast into their homes every night.)

Parents have many unresolved issues they may have been addressing, or not addressing. After all, they were also raised by human beings, as were their parents, and so on and so on, back a few million years. We're all susceptible to bad imprinting because most of the humans we've been raised by have been subjected to the same flawed parenting.

Whether the issue is an unhappy marriage, substance abuse problems, psychological issues such as depression and obsessive compulsive disorders, or a multitude of other issues, there are likely adult issues affecting the children's feelings of security and worth, and as a result, their lifelong self-esteem. Adults often compensate for the issues of their early development, and sometimes not in the healthiest ways, and the result is a ripple effect through generations.

Young children have no choice in the environment in which they live. They're stuck with whatever neurotic world their parents and society have created for them. With their parents, it's those unresolved neuroses that are passed on, and the child is forced to adapt to them. With society, it's the craving for money, status and importance that create an unhealthy environment, and the emphasis on an extreme busyness that often doesn't allow them to live or properly connect with others. With all of our modern devices, from e-mail to cell phones, there's a common perception that we're better connected.

But it's an incorrect premise: we aren't connected electronically in addition to being connected personally. We're connected electronically instead of personally, and that human contact can't be replaced.

Chuck that substitution!

You have choices in how you live, and the world won't stop spinning if you don't answer that call or e-mail. It's better, in fact, if things spin a little slower sometimes. Often we're the novelty act from the old *Ed Sullivan Show*, spinning plates on sticks, frantically racing back and forth between the wobbling plates.

But we know how that act always ends: the plates hit the floor and break, no matter how hard the man races back and forth. After all, he can't run forever.

Neither can you.

And your every action sets a tone and sends a message to your children: life is hectic and out of control; you can only be happy if you're in perpetual motion; there's no life in living, only endless activities; enjoyment is something to be postponed after everything else is done.

I couldn't outrun my problems, and you can't spin plates forever. Set the proper tone for your life and the lives you influence most—those of your children—and address your issues and learn to stop running or spinning or texting or e-mailing. Take a breath and enjoy life.

By the way, that feeling that you were a bad parent because you set the wrong tone or sent the wrong message at times: Chuck It!

Most parents do the best they're capable of doing and aren't even aware of the issues they accidentally subject their children to. Yes, there are parents who are deliberately cruel, which is totally unforgivable, but most parents (particularly parents who are sufficiently in touch with their own emotions that they might question their parenting skills) err out of human fallibility, not on the side of brutality.

That's the benefit of counseling, coaching and mentoring. It exposes us to healthy ways of living, unmasks the roots behind our issues, and with the proper counseling, these healthy approaches to living become reinforced, creating new habits in the place of the damaged reflexes.

For those unfamiliar with the process, counseling doesn't initially involve anything more complicated than listening. Everyone has a need to tell his story, and everyone has a story. If you're curious about human beings in general, like I am, you realize this on a daily basis. Most people, with time on their hands and some gentle prompting, will tell you their story. It might not be the story of their childhood, or what scared or scarred them, but it will be a story that reveals something important to them: an achievement, a failure, a journey, a loss.

And don't be afraid: they're not looking to be cured by you; they simply want someone to listen to them.

Counseling begins at that simple level—listening—but unlike your mother or husband or neighbor, counselors have no biases or preconceived notions about who you are. They're confidential, and they're trained to listen empathetically. That's the beginning, and it's simple and secure and comfortable…the things childhood was supposed to be, but probably wasn't.

We've reached an era where (despite the occasional clichéd media portrayals of psychologists as being crazy or irresponsible) counseling no longer carries a stigma. Asking for help isn't weak; it's probably the bravest thing we ever do.

Chuck that fear!

And caring, responsible people want to be able to help others. Follow the advice of the flight attendants on commercial airlines: don't attempt to put the oxygen mask on your children until you've affixed your own first. It's difficult to help others; t's difficult to parent well or engage in healthy relationships, until you feel good about *yourself* first.

That was what I had intended from day one of my professional life—helping people feel good about themselves—and my business had taken off because it was meeting a real need; from the moment I opted to see a counselor, I had finally made that same commitment to helping *myself*.

In my business, we often work with people with severe problems, but sometimes, we work with people whose greatest problem is poor self-image and poor self-esteem, and all they may need is a gentle push in the right direction.

We all encounter people like this every day: the kid playing baseball who gets a fluke hit and, believing in himself for the first time, suddenly starts pounding the ball; or the student who scores well on a difficult test and, realizing that she's smarter than she thought, pulls up *all* her grades. For most of us, merely being put in a position to succeed is enough. It's getting that opportunity that can be daunting.

One of my clients in Chicago had a nephew who came from a dysfunctional family and couldn't seem to get his life started, and she asked if I could help him, even though any assistance I provided was outside the EAP plan for the company. I agreed to help.

She explained that in this young man's family, there was a history of physical abuse and alcoholism, and the young man still lived with his mother. Years of therapy had done little to improve his situation.

I met him at the Midway Airport in Chicago and found Mike to a very likable young man in his twenties. He appeared to have very little self-esteem, and told me that he still lived at home, was on disability, had no social life and felt extremely alienated from people around him. So I began a process of counseling over the phone, but as with his prior therapy, there didn't seem to be much improvement.

So I thought of a unique way to try to reach him. I was presenting a training seminar for one of my clients in Chicago and I called and asked Mike to pick me up at the airport. I told him I needed a ride to the seminar, and invited him to sit in on the training if he wanted.

The session was a supervisory training, and when I walked in, I introduced Mike to the people there as one of my assistants. Right away, Mike sat up in the chair. I think I had taken him by surprise, and I definitely had his attention.

In the middle of the seminar, I asked him an easy question that just required a "yes" response. He said "yes," and sat up even taller in the chair. He now was my assistant as far as those in attendance knew.

After the workshop, he told me how impressed he was with my presentation, and how much he enjoyed being introduced and contributing, even in that small way.

"You know, I feel better about myself. I think I can do this," he said.

"Good, because I know you can do this," I told him. Since that day, Mike has come off disability, has moved out of his mother's house and bought has his own home, has married and has a daughter and a terrific job at a computer company.

Am I overestimating the effect my confidence in him had? We still keep in touch ten years later, and he identifies that day in Chicago as the turning point with his life. That little acknowledgment, that unexpected feeling of worthiness had kick-started his self-esteem.

Closer to home, I had an employee named Sophia whose

daughter was a pleasant girl, but developmentally challenged and rather overweight, and obviously lacking in confidence. There had been problems at home with her father, and this girl had suffered for it psychologically. She needed a job, Sophia explained, and there were few opportunities for her besides minimum wage, so I hired her.

She turned out to be good with numbers; in fact, she turned out to be great with numbers. Gradually, at work, her demeanor changed. She dressed better, slimmed down, started wearing makeup and became more outgoing. Eventually, she was promoted to a supervisor's position in the finance department with a good salary and benefits.

Since she worked in a building filled with therapists, she received good support and advice. (And our therapists all generally see therapists because we all see on a daily basis the value of therapy, so it's a very supportive work environment.) She began to date for the first time, and sometime after was engaged.

One day, she mentioned that her fiancé was from Larchmont, New York. I've only ever known one family from Larchmont, that of my first accountant, Sheldon Horowitz. Sheldon and his wife would come and sit on the floor of my 42nd Street apartment and do my books, and I'd kept Sheldon on after he'd had a heart attack and had his pacemaker installed. When all his other clients had dropped him I'd kept Sheldon on out of loyalty, and because he was a good man, and he continued to work for me until he passed away nearly twenty-four years ago.

"I used to know a Sheldon Horowitz from Larchmont," I said.

"My fiancé is named Daniel Horowitz," she replied.

That blossoming young lady, who I had come to love like a

daughter, had indeed married the son of my first accountant. She had come so far with some simple encouragement, and her transformation from the chubby, shy girl with low self-esteem to a supervisor with a husband, a home and a very satisfying life, is a visible reminder to me every day of how the smallest gestures can have far-reaching effects.

Chapter Twelve
Fighting Dis-ease

The Unfolding

We cannot love
if our pace
is too rapid
or
our eyes too hard.

We can,
if we move slowly
together,
and observe the
gentle unfolding
of the flowers
along our path.

In ancient Greece, physicians were only paid if their patients were healthy. Imagine if that principle were in effect today? Would your doctor merit being paid, or do you feel as though you're on an assembly line and that asking questions interferes with business? (To be fair, the healthcare industry squeezes doctors almost as badly as it squeezes patients, but that shouldn't be your cross to bear.) Modern physicians have less motivation than ever to keep people healthy and less time to properly treat each patient, and the array of pharmacological solutions many of them prescribe often mask problems or numb pain without resolving the underlying problem.

A lot of us suffer from "dis-ease" these days; literally, we're not at ease. People think of disease as something that afflicts the body; dis-ease is an affliction of the mind, and it's entirely treatable.

But we shouldn't medicate ourselves with drugs or alcohol to treat dis-ease. It's no surprise people self-medicate, because human beings have always self-medicated. The modern spin on self-medication is that people are *encouraged* to self-medicate. Can't get at the source of your depression or compulsive behavior! Take a pill! Your problem is that you take too many pills? Take a different pill!

Modern science and medicine have taught us that easy solutions are available, and with all the pressure to get things done quickly, there's no time to wait for results from a prolonged effort. Sometimes, there's no time for any effort. So we reach for the quickest resolution without considering the underlying cause, or a permanent, un-medicated answer to the problem.

And how often does the alleged cure create yet another problem? We're not very good at self-medicating, statistics prove, because we're susceptible to addiction and compulsion, and sometimes we make bad choices—people who drink because they're depressed, for example, even though alcohol is a depressant.

It's understandable that people are overwhelmed. Modern life is complicated. It was the nineteenth century when William

Wordsworth wrote, "The world is too much with us; late and soon, Getting and spending, we lay waste our powers..." Life has become considerably more complex in the two centuries since those words were written. Everywhere we turn, there is noise, interruptions and conflict, and the one thing our subconscious mind (and very often our conscious mind) craves is some quiet time to sort things out.

I was in the airport in St. Louis when I noticed an elderly man lying on sofa on a balcony. He wasn't homeless, but he certainly looked overwhelmed. I approached him (I'm still a born caregiver, just not to a degree that's destructive) and I asked if I could be of assistance.

He said his flight had been cancelled and he couldn't read the small print telling how to catch a cab, and he was too embarrassed to ask anyone. So overwhelming was the experience of being stranded in the airport with nowhere to stay that he opted to curl up on a couch. So, I got on the phone, booked him a hotel room and sent for a cab to come pick him up. He was grateful, and I was glad I had been there to help.

The old man wasn't suffering from dementia; he wasn't lost and he wasn't poor. He was just overwhelmed. Not only that, but hundreds of people walked past and either didn't see him or opted not to ask, even though he was clearly overwhelmed by his predicament. He was suffering acute dis-ease, and all that was required to cure it was the human connection, but it was missing.

Sometimes, we're all stranded at the airport without a room. Life is too much with us, and we need time to think, to breathe and relax. An obsession with work or constant communication and information leaves no room for actual living, and the world will intrude as much as you allow it to.

That lifestyle? Chuck It!

You can be a success and still feel good about yourself, and you can work hard and still take time to smell the flowers, play with the kids, walk the dog and talk with a friend. I know it can be done, because I do it every day. Not that I'm big on vacations; actually, I get restless and bored very quickly on vacation. But then, I like my job, and I don't see it as a task but as a puzzle, and it's a joy to me on a daily basis to help people, to interact with clients and employees and friends, and to run my benevolent kingdom with the goal of benefiting as many people as possible.

But I fit in my down time every single day, whether it's meditation or reading or working at the animal shelter or simply staring out a window and watching people as I pet my cats. Every day for me requires some play and some work; any less balance and I feel like the puzzle isn't complete.

I try to live my life backwards, with the perspective of an old man evaluating his decisions in retrospect. What meant more to me: saving those orphaned ducks that were trying to cross the highway or finishing my lunch and making it the airport on time? One has no monetary value attached to it but a feeling of relief and satisfaction instead; the other has a specific dollar value but no emotional value.

Don't place more importance on arbitrary deadlines over finding time for yourself, and don't sacrifice your quiet time, your daily mini-vacations of the mind, for another phone call or e-mail.

Chuck those priorities and make YOU a priority.

We can't live a life of ease until we learn to dispense with the dis-ease.

Chapter Thirteen
How We Can Help

The Gift

Before leaving for the hospital,
he hung a beautiful plant with
tiny flowers
that would soon blossom.

He would not be home
for Mother's Day.
But the gift
would bloom at that time.

What is an employee assistance program?

I've been using the term throughout this book, and I know some people know what it means and others have actually used one. But I should clarify what an EAP is, what we do as a provider of such services and how we're different from other EAP providers.

Saying "an EAP is like" is akin to describing the taste of curry. Yes, we know basically what it should be like, that it should care for employee physical and mental health needs, but as each curry is specific to the dish it's prepared for, and it's prepared from scratch, each EAP should be tailored for the company it serves. Like a masterful Indian cook's approach to making curry, we tailor our services to each company's specific needs.

The EAP is a confidential counseling and referral service for employees and their household members, contracted and prepaid for by the employer, available twenty-four hours a day, seven days a week via the telephone. The EAP also has an office that's convenient to the workplace and a comprehensive network of licensed psychologists, social workers, alcohol and drug counselors, marriage and family counselors, eldercare and childcare providers.

Areas that the EAP can provide help with include family/parenting issues, grief and bereavement issues, marital and relationship issues, legal/financial issues, stress and anxiety issues, depression, drug and alcohol problems, or any other personal problem.

Sometimes we even tailor to individual needs, but more on that later.

Let's revisit my first big client, the Golden Nugget Casino. There are no industries with the same exact issues as the gaming industry. There are some that are close, of course. Airlines, for example, once placed strict weight restrictions on flight attendants, like casinos have on their waitresses; some restaurants are open all night like a casino, but very few. Some industries have a high percentage of substance abuse (air traffic controllers come to mind), but casinos deal every day with addicted people in addition to employing some addicted people (as all industries do). Plus, industries like geriatric or hospice care have constant contact with the elderly, as do casinos, but don't encounter issues prevalent in casinos to the same degree.

In other words, EAP isn't a one-size-fits-all industry, although my competitors often have no problem trying to squeeze the nasty stepsister's thorny foot into Cinderella's glass slipper.

We customize services for each client, and I'm always looking for ways to improve and help our clients, from counseling and work-life programs to any other area where we believe we can add value.

For example, we provide managed mental health carve out programs, where we take the behavioral component out of a self-insured plan and managed it the way it should be managed: for service, quality of care and savings. With the EAP on the front end and an integrated managed program on the back end, we have saved our clients as much as thirty-five to forty percent in mental health costs while providing the employees the care they need.

We also work with our clients' workers' compensation staff to provide mental health support and training. We've developed a patient advocate program so employees and family members can better understand their benefits and services and how to navigate the system to get the proper care.

It's not much use to have terrific care options if you don't know how to use them.

We have also developed pharmacy programs for clients, though I'm certain that many people, instead of using medication, could benefit from counseling, exercise, healthy eating and continued coaching. Medicine is essential when it treats an illness, but as I stated earlier, medication is often a shortcut used to mask symptoms or dull psychological pain. Counseling gets at the root of the issue, and while it's an ongoing process that can take time to reap its ultimate rewards, it can bring about remarkable and healthy changes for committed individuals.

I envision a day when counseling is an integral part of all healthcare plans and all stigma has been removed, but first, we need to wean ourselves off the medicine-cures-all approach to healthcare.

We also developed an eldercare specialty so employees can address the needs of their aging family members, a growing segment of the population. People need the proper information, support and coaching so they can make informed choices regarding their decisions, about their relatives and themselves. Our eldercare counselors take the time to get to know our clients and their specific needs.

Getting to know the clients sets us apart as well.

In an age where electronic communication is the only human contact some people have, we still provide the human touch, the kindness, thoughtfulness and care that can't be simulated by vicarious contact. Whether it's a crisis like Hurricane Katrina, where our counselors worked out of trailers servicing clients in the Gulf, or in a possible pandemic such as the bird flu, or in the midst of a violent catastrophe like 9/11, where we provided immediate service for our clients as well as counseling for the clergy who worked at Ground Zero, we tailor the response to the issues and immediacy of the situation.

A member of the clergy asked me advice on servicing the needs of the 9/11 survivor families, as well as his congregation, which was traumatized by the event, living as close as they were to the Twin Towers. I told him to really "be present," which meant meeting with each and every person who needs him and listening to their issues and providing comfort, and being like a laser beam, completely focused on the person or people he was counseling. I told him not to look at his watch or the person walking by, or think about what he had to do later. There's no multi-tasking with this much emotional trauma to address.

This "being present," laser beam approach is much more exhausting than regular counseling. It's actually more exhausting than exercising at the gym. Focusing on someone's pain and fear is an art, and an art you put your all into it, every second.

But that wasn't the end of the advice, of course, because clergymen and other caregivers need someone to talk to, particularly after such emotionally exhausting work. So, I advised him to get his own counseling or coaching, and in the end, we provided a confidential assistant program to aid the caregivers associated with 9/11.

It's our responsibility to "be present" with the people we service as well. Counseling provides tremendous support and a terrific alternative to medication, which is much overused and has many unhealthy side effects. Counseling takes time, though, and patience and thinking; you can't push a button like on a cell phone and have your answers, but it's the most effective and least expensive kind of assistance around, and better than any pill.

We also work with businesses that have occasional traumatic events, so when there's a robbery at a client like, say, Barnes & Noble Books, we provide crisis counseling for their staff onsite. It was these small incidents that enabled us to mobilize for larger events like 9/11 or Hurricane Katrina. Similarly, when one client had a disgruntled doctor enter the emergency room at one of its medical centers, we provided around-the-clock care for the those employees who had to continue to work at the hospital, who hadn't been directly affected but who nonetheless had been shaken by the experience.

With another client, Service Corporation International, which is the largest funeral home company in the country, we came up with the idea for a compassion helpline for people who purchased a dignity plan, which was sold either pre-need or at-need. The plan was an invaluable service for people who had a loved one die, or who needed information regarding counseling services.

Too often, we're told that there's a grieving process when we lose a loved one, but we're not sure how that process works. (Even people with happy childhoods and good imprinting may need assistance coping with the loss of a loved one.) We have provided counseling to thousands of people with this service, and they have access to the counseling service anytime, twenty-four hours a day, three hundred sixty-five days a year.

I spoke with a woman who had been widowed after fifty-one years of marriage, and she resented being told by friends and family to "keep busy."

"I don't want to keep busy," she explained. "I just want to be left alone to grieve."

We all grieve in our own fashion, and it's not for others to dictate how, or how long. People need to know it's okay to feel what they feel, and that feeling can change not just day to day but hour to hour. The important thing is for them to express their sorrow. Those who don't grieve carry a heavy burden.

So it's our committed job to do what it takes to counsel our clients. All they have to do is provide us access so we can determine what they need, and we develop a protocol to fit their needs.

Our clients receive access from our service via our twenty-four-hour counseling line staffed only by master's degree counselors ands PhDs. We want every caller to receive excellent customer service and to immediately speak to a therapist, if that's what they need. Callers want to tell their stories one time, and not to a system determined to triage services, and in some cases meant to deny services entirely.

There are EAPs that actually discourage callers, that intentionally complicate the process in hope that the callers give up. The rationale here, as with every profit-driven service industry, is to only provide service when it's demanded. It sounds at odds with the idea of healthcare, but believe it, there are companies whose goal is to deny the caller service, and you can picture the justification: "If they wanted it bad enough, they would be persistent."

I wish we could Chuck that philosophy as a culture, but it's prevalent in healthcare these days.

First of all, you shouldn't have to plead with your health services to provide you with what they're paid to provide you. Second, not everyone has the psychological stamina or self-esteem to fight through a maze of phone prompts, indifferent triage services and argumentative phone reps. Maybe those issues are the reason they're calling in the first place. "I have trouble being assertive... Hello? I think they hung up on me..."

We don't operate that way. We welcome every client and do whatever it takes to solve their problem, whether it's substance abuse, marital issues, problem with a child, grief issues, work problems, relationships or depression. We want all employees to know we are there for them, and no problem is too small. They're all that man at Credit Lyonaisse to me, the focus of our attention for as long as they need us.

Does providing better care and individualized service hurt my bottom line?

Of course! I may not be a natural businessman, but I recognize policies and behavior that don't enhance our profitability.

Do I provide those services anyway?

Of course! I am always willing to sacrifice money to give better quality and service, as long as the true bottom line—that everyone in my employ (including me) is being adequately compensated as well—remains intact. Going out of business because I'm selfless to the point of self-destruction doesn't benefit anyone. I'm okay with growing slowly and carefully managing the company's growth so we continue to give impeccable service.

My staff coordinates care and service to my network of more than twenty thousand clinicians nationwide. It would be easier to staff without the master's level and graduate training, and less expensive, but I want the best for the people who use our services and for the companies where they work. Squeezing extra money from the equation and sacrificing quality may be good for the bottom line short-term (though long-term, I sincerely doubt it), but it's bad math for the soul.

How far are we willing to go to provide customized service? I'll give several examples of how far I'm willing to go, which set an example for my employees, who understand that my bottom line is not about dollars and cents.

I remember a call I took on our counseling line. (I still spend a quarter of my time at work on the counseling phones, because it gives me fulfillment and reminds me why I wanted to be in this business to begin with.) The call was from a man in Chicago who had a father in Jersey City, New Jersey, who was going through a terminal illness. The father, a veteran flyer who had served with the famed Tuskegee Airmen during World War II, was accustomed to being very self-sufficient and was too proud to call the employee assistance program and ask for counseling. The airman's wife was having an extremely difficult time with the illness and the seriousness of the situation had now reached his son in Chicago.

I thought about a solution to this dilemma and came to a conclusion: why not make a house call?

Those of you under age fifty might not recall house calls, but they're not a myth. Once upon a time, doctors actually visited the homes of patients. I know, it's a stunning concept, particularly when your doctor probably needs your chart in his hand to even recall your name and what he prescribed for you last year, but I remember the practice from my youth and recall that it often achieved excellent results.

So I drove to Kennedy Boulevard in Jersey City, knocked on the door of the house and was greeted with lovely smiles by this charming couple. I found that Mr. Scott had not only been an airman, but a highly respected judge in Jersey City. He was accustomed to being very self-sufficient and working hard, and was a person I judged to be of great integrity. I told him why I had come, that his son was concerned about him, and we talked and talked: about his life, his family, his career as a judge, World War II, and how he loved to golf but was saddened that he couldn't do it anymore because of his illness.

I had a thought: maybe he couldn't golf outside on the course, but he could certainly practice putting in the house. We took a coffee mug, placed it on its side and we both practiced putting. It was great fun for me, and we did it again many more times, practicing putting as we talked about philosophy, about the meaning of life, what it was like for him being black during the war, about the old Jersey City and his favorite diner, Al's. Judge Scott and I remained friends until he passed away.

I look back to on our many meetings with fondness. I'm happy that I could get to know a fine and interesting man better; I'm pleased that we had many laughs and good times, and I hope my visits made reaching the end of his life more pleasurable for him.

You needn't be a psychologist to provide that service to an elderly or ill person. And I can't personally serve every client I know to that degree. But I can do it often enough to remind myself that the human touch sparks something within me, and that spark ignites something in those I touch.

Another call I received was from a retiree who had worked for one of my clients. This woman, Agnes, became a regular who called weekly until she died. Though she was from North Carolina and I was in New Jersey, she would mail baked items to me and my office staff. I always looked forward to her calls and to hearing her cheerful voice, and I loved knowing that retired employees like her were using our counseling helpline.

First of all, the retirees are the people who've built the company and should never be forgotten. Secondly, these are people who in many cases have lost their spouses and most of their peers, and need someone to talk with. Lastly, seniors have a high incidence of depression and substance abuse because the loneliness can be so frustrating, and they're often forgotten as a demographic that needs our assistance, not just through EAPs but as a culture.

So I learned long ago to keep an eye out for our clients' retirees, or the parents of the employees. I always like to get a list of the company retirees and have my staff call them and see how they are. We know from past experience that these individuals love getting our calls and always have a story to tell, and we're happy to lend an ear.

Similarly, when clients have layoffs, I like to have our staff call the employees and see how they and their family are doing. I remember a chemist who was laid off and was so pleased to receive our call. He mentioned how his son saw his dad work hard and get laid off, and was going through a crisis—he didn't want to study in school. What was the use of working hard if they just dump you when they no longer need you?

Our counselors talked to the boy about change being a scary but potentially positive thing during a few counseling sessions, and sure enough, his dad got another job and he realized that when you persevere, you can adapt to a difficult situation and turn it into a positive experience.

The counseling was very important, of course, but back to the imprinting issue we've already discussed: seeing his dad persevere and get another job probably did as much for the boy's confidence as anything we could say.

Then there was Joseph, a builder of hotels and office buildings, from Westchester, New York. His wife of sixty-five years had recently died and he wanted to share the story of his life and connect again to those beautiful memories. I allowed him to understand that it's all right to feel those feelings, the almost unbearable feelings of loss and sadness. It was okay to feel what he was feeling, and I was right there with him, so he could feel and together we could eventually heal.

Though Joseph was very wealthy, he said his favorite times (and his wife had always agreed) was when they were living in a studio apartment in Greenwich Village in New York City and he was just building his business. The homes he'd been able to buy and the money he'd made actually meant very little to him. But having time, seeing his wife smile, the struggles they had endured and the dreams they had shared for the life together, those meant the world to him. (It's no longer surprising to me that people recall their years of struggling with fondness; money doesn't buy happiness, we know, and poverty ensures a simplicity of life that affluence often complicates.)

I couldn't fix his sorrow, and he didn't expect me to fix it. He just wanted to share the story of his life with me, and to move on with his grieving.

Sometimes that's all a customer needs, and sometimes, it's all a friend needs.

And you may surprise yourself one day and strike up a conversation with a complete stranger and discover that you both feel better when you walk away.

Chapter Fourteen
The Third Act

Waterlilly

She goes to the pond everyday.
For about an hour she watches
one water lily.

No one understands why
or
what she is looking at for so long.
They only know,
she is neither
a painter,
a poet,
nor a botanist.

One day,
She did not return to the pond.
So I decided to venture near the water
and silently observe.

> I remained for some time.
> Just observing
> watching one water lily
> on the pond.

So I had reached a point in my life where most of what I had reached for, I had achieved, both personally and professionally.

If this were a novel, this is the point in the story where the protagonist, having overcome obstacles and reached his goal, would suffer a personal or professional setback, or lose his way and move to Tahiti and party his days away. The third act requires some resolution of the crisis, usually a positive one: how does our hero rediscover his love for a) the life he left behind, b) the good woman who truly loves him, or c) the culture or people he abandoned in his climb to the top?

The crisis that would precipitate my third act would be less dramatic than that, but no less significant to me.

Running a business properly requires constant nurturing. As of this writing, we are the eighth-largest EAP company in the United States, with nine hundred corporate clients and more than four million people enrolled, and we continue to grow. We are one of the only large EAP companies that is still private. The large public companies often come knocking to buy my business.

Every time I wonder…should I sell it? But I'm having too much fun. There may be a time when I would sell, perhaps if the purchasing company can continue the service we developed and maintain integrity. But there isn't enough money in the world to make me hand over those clients to just another profit-driven company.

Our culture equates size with quality, and we equate earnings with good business. No one sets out to fail in business, and no one hopes to make less than their competitors. After several years, I had reached a size where I could still manage the business hands-on, and that gave me joy. But even if I didn't want my business to become larger (which I did), I still had incentive to make it better.

And I still had some lessons to learn, such as how a little adversity will help you reassess your beliefs, and possibly realign your mission.

Invariably, with business and life, no matter how much you prepare, or the precautions you take, things will still go wrong and change, both positive and negative, is the only constant in life. But don't fear change! The measure of our lives is making constant adjustments, and trying to deny that only creates a very bumpy ride.

Years ago, someone did a study of centenarians, or people who'd lived a hundred years or more. These people came from every economic background, every race, and had a variety of jobs and life experiences, and in some cases, had endured tragedies. In the end, the researcher could find only one thing in common among them: they all handled adversity uncommonly well. They accepted that change was inevitable, and that loss was a necessary part of life. They were able to mourn, feel and then moved froward with their lives.

In a hurricane, it's not the mightiest oak that necessarily survives: it's the plant that can bend with the wind, and after the storm, the blades of grass are still standing while the mighty oak has been pulled out by its roots.

In business and in life, we are all tested repeatedly, sometimes to the degree that the core of the business is shaken, as well as our belief in the goodness of people. That doesn't mean our business is inherently fallible, that our plan is flawed or that people are inherently bad. It's merely a reminder that there will always be challenges to our core beliefs and professional and personal security.

My business plan wasn't MBA-inspired; I wasn't a businessman by design. I'm a psychologist seeking to provide quality care to the maximum number of people. I'm a businessman because that's the best path for my dream. In fact, in the first year that my accountant, Sheldon Horowitz, did my books, he discovered that I hadn't paid my quarterly taxes to the federal government.

Quarterly taxes? I was accustomed to someone taking those out of my paycheck for me.

A bigger surprise occurred in my sixth year of being in business. My company had been hired to provide the EAP for one of the largest food companies in the United States. This company had approximately thirty thousand employees in locations throughout the country, so it took us two years to successfully tailor a program to their needs, visit all the work sites and provide training to all the employees, supervisors, plant managers, union members and corporate office employees and executives.

I personally made sure the quality of the training was superb, all the clinicians were in place, and everything was communicated properly. The program was a monumental success, feedback was excellent and employee utilization was outstanding. I even became good friends with the company liaison who was in charge of the program, since we usually traveled together and had the opportunity to get to know each other quite well.

In addition to the services we provided, I also provided this liaison with a special caretaker for his father, who had Alzheimer's, and special counseling for his daughter, who was ill with cancer.

In other words, we had fulfilled our end of the bargain, and then some. But sometimes things go awry, and human nature reveals its darker side.

The EAP we were providing was receiving excellent feedback and reviews. We provided many types of wellness workshops for them, as well as special supervisory leadership training seminars, and we intervened when there were union and management conflicts. We were on the spot with crisis management, and went above and beyond with service, which I try to do with every client. (Every client, remember, is as important as that one disenfranchised employee at Credit Lyonnais.) Besides the EAP service, I also wanted to provide them with industrial psychologists to address such issues such as downsizing, acquisitions and hiring.

We were making things work for that client. It was the perfect provider/client relationship: I gained their business and they received excellent service in return.

In the fourth year of service, a strange thing happened.

Suddenly, one of their locations opted out of the service. So I asked the company liaison, who I was now good friends with, why.

"Don't be alarmed," he said. "We're just trying an experiment, working with a couple of guys who are compiling the statistics for me."

I accepted this explanation, except one at a time, little by little, other sites also began to opt out of our services.

Now I was very concerned.

So I again tried to contact my friend and got no reply. Then I contacted his assistant, who was no help.

So I visited one of the locations that had opted for the change. I approached the human resources manager in a friendly manner, and he showed me numbers from my friend's the statistic compilers, showing that utilization was low, which was why the company liaison wanted to change vendors.

That would have been understandable if it was true. But I compared the numbers he showed me with the actual number of how many people we paid to provide service to their employees. The discrepancy was huge. The liaison's stat compilers had altered the statistics!

Welcome to the ugly side of the business world, Chuck!

By then, it was too late for me to fix the problem. The icing on the cake (and this is not a cake *anyone* would want to eat) was that the company liaison and the two fellows from the statistics group had formed their own employee assistance company and had taken the entire client with them.

After I'd discovered their maneuver, the company liaison—my "friend"—called me to say he felt bad about what he'd done. With their one stolen client, they went out and tried to obtain businesses on their own, but after a few years, they could no longer even service their original client, and they began to argue amongst themselves and were finally compelled to sell off their small, fledging business.

Some years later, the company liaison called me and said that I'd made running a business look so easy, he'd thought he could do it...that is, until he'd realized the immense work it entailed—the marketing, reporting, servicing, training, preparation, attention to detail, legal and financial issues, just to name a few

"It wasn't as easy as it looked," he admitted. But I already knew that.

It's nice to know that good practices can inspire others. But it's another sensation altogether to realize that your good work has inspired someone you trust to undermine you.

Karma is sweet, though. (For those of you unfamiliar with karma, it's the Buddhist principle that the way you act toward others comes back to you eventually...and it surely does.) The liaison and his statistics cohorts went out of business in less than two years, and they were only providing service to the one client they stole away from me. (Incidentally, the darker, less appealing cousin to karma is *schadenfreude*, that guilty pleasure we get from seeing someone else's misfortune. Not that I experienced *schadenfreude*, but I certainly would've been within my rights.)

I didn't see his unscrupulous maneuver coming. Not having been raised or educated in a business environment, I expected most people to be genuine in how they represented themselves, and I'd thought the liaison had integrity and would be honest with me, particularly after I'd befriended him and helped his family. But, I was reminded that some people are capable of rationalizing in their own minds what is right and justifying it to themselves.

How else could he sleep at night? I know I would've been wracked by guilt, and I know I'm not the only person with that kind of conscience.

At the time, it was a difficult loss, and because of it I had to let some employees go, which was personally painful. In running my business I'm not only providing a service to the client, I'm providing a means of support and opportunities for my employees. Letting people go, even though it wasn't my fault and certainly wasn't what I wanted, was still painful.

The entire episode was a learning experience about human nature in general and business in particular. Sometimes, despite your best efforts, things go wrong. Sometimes it may even be your fault. But guilt is a wasted emotion, and regret solves nothing.

Chuck those thoughts!

Learn from the mistakes and problems you encounter. A cynic might say that I had learned not to trust people, but that's not my nature, and that's not what most of my encounters teach me about people. I still trust my instinct when it comes to individuals and feel optimistic about humanity in general. Life has enough adversity without your being suspicious of everyone's motives, and while that trust makes you vulnerable, it also makes you accessible, empathetic and thoroughly human.

Being trusted by others requires trust on your part, after all.

What I learned instead is that just because I think I'm doing a good job, it doesn't guarantee that good things will happen. In fact, sometimes the person who is best at something fails repeatedly. That doesn't mean their vision is misguided or their methods are incorrect, or that it's a sign that they should give up.

As baseball players are known to say, "I hit that pitch exactly the way I wanted to. Once it leaves my bat, I have no control over where it goes."

I'd done my best, I'd been undermined, and I felt wronged. But it didn't inspire vengeful thoughts or make me question my motives, because I'd done everything the right way. I wasn't deterred; if anything, I was recommitted to providing the best possible service I could to as many people as I could reach.

So take your swings and remember that everyone, even the best among us, strikes out once in a while. Sometimes you can even hit the ball over the fence, and the centerfielder reaches up and pulls it back.

That applies to our personal lives as well. That failed relationship that just ended? Maybe you weren't a good match. Or maybe you were a good match but someone or something got in the way. Maybe you didn't try hard enough, or maybe she didn't. (Bad relationships are easy; good relationships can be a lot of work.) Maybe one of you just gave up. (It doesn't require two consenting individuals to sabotage a relationship.)

If every relationship in your life is difficult, it's time for introspection: it's not everyone else, it's you. But you can be a caring and compassionate person who makes an effort to empathize with others and still have a relationship you care about go south.

What will your third act be? Will that crisis send you to a Tahiti of the mind, no longer making the effort in your work or in your personal life, or will you use the setback to change course, or even reverse direction?

Or, will it inspire you to refocus and recommit to your goals? And your goals needn't be Earth-shattering, by the way. They only need to be important to you.

F. Scott Fitzgerald claimed that there are no second acts in American lives, but I dispute that premise, and not just because he was a cynic who died young without earning his chance at a second act. We're all capable of second and third acts and even more, as long as we don't let the occasional setback derail us from our quest.

Chapter Fifteen
Making Choices

Perspective

He thought
life was a goal
to be achieved.

If he came
to a stream,
he crossed it.

Now when he
comes to the stream,
he floats in it.

And what a difference
that makes.

Motivation can be a temporary state of mind.
    Let's say you've decided to lose twenty pounds, and this time you're *very* determined. So you buy the diet book that's

the current rage and you seriously set to following the path it lays out for you. And the path is very restrictive: let's say, just for fun, it's the cabbage diet (which was actually a fad diet decades ago), which states that you can eat as much cabbage as you want as often as you want, but nothing else for thirty days. It says that the pounds will melt away and you'll purify your system while you're at it.

So you begin consuming cabbage. A lot of cabbage. What you discover is that there are relatively few ways to prepare cabbage, minus the boiled corned beef or gobs of mayonnaise, that makes it taste like—well, food. (Cabbage lovers, and you know who you are, shouldn't take this personally, as there are also people who enjoy haggis and Brussel sprouts out there.) In fact, the entire experience is nauseating, and your house stinks of cabbage and your family declines to eat meals within a hundred yards of you, but as long as you're losing weight, the entire wretched experience is tolerable.

I'm going to look great when this is over, you tell yourself. *I can live without enjoying what I eat for a while.*

And at the end of the week—a long, culinary wasteland of a week—you step on the scale and see that…you haven't lost a single pound.

Your motivation has deflated. So you give up the cabbage diet, which even a rabbit couldn't survive on. (Even rabbits require some balance to their diet and considerably less fiber.) And you resign yourself, at least until the next fad diet comes along, or the New Year's resolution list, to carrying the extra twenty pounds.

If this sounds familiar, it should, because most dieters don't stay on their diets, and most diets fail. In fact, the vast majority of "fix it quick" ideas don't work for the vast majority of people.

It's because we're weak, we tell ourselves. It's because we're undisciplined, and we're destined to remain twenty pounds overweight for the rest of our lives. We blame ourselves for failing to follow an illogical and unbalanced plan that's been sold to us as a cure for our problem, and being overweight is not only unhealthy, it's a visible stigma that our society feels free to ridicule.

But it's ridiculous to feel that way about the twenty pounds, of course. You'll probably gain even *more* weight as you get older. (Were you really expecting an empty platitude that would verbally remove the extra twenty pounds?) And your only failing was in putting faith in an empty promise that's been sold as science.

There are very few quick fixes in life that work, and our mental health in this regard is no different than our physical health.

What do quick fixes address? Like most medications for physical or emotional pain, they tend to address symptoms, not the source of the problem, and what side effects do these medications cause? What are you left with when the symptoms subside and the medication runs out?

The same problem you started with.

Modern life discourages moderation and long-term planning. A real diet, for example, is something you can follow for life, or at least until allergies or illness alter it or eliminate certain elements from it. But a healthy diet is built on the ideal of balance and moderation, not on bingeing and fad dieting the excess weight away. As unhealthy as the original food pyramid was, even its creators, who were in the thrall of the beef and dairy industries, didn't envision a culture where so many people get such a high percentage of their calories in fried nugget form, or try to remove the additional pounds by eating unbalanced and illogical food combinations.

Eating healthy requires disciple, just like working toward a personal goal. Nothing worthwhile is achieved without some effort. Saying you can't do something when you haven't tried is both self-defeating and incorrect.

We are all self-made. Only those who have succeeded are willing to admit it.

Chuck that negativity!

If you're truly interested in living healthier and not yo-yoing your weight, then visit a nutritionist and learn how to combine balanced meals with moderate exercise. You'll never need another fad diet as long as you live.

And maybe you'll never lose that twenty pounds. But are you healthy? Are you comfortable with yourself? Would losing the twenty pounds add anything to your life?

Maybe that's what you're meant to weigh, and if you're living healthy and you're otherwise content with your life, there are bigger problems to have than twenty extra pounds.

Oh, and shouldn't our parents have taught us to eat healthy? (Some of them did and we declined to listen.) Of course they should have, but we're back to that negative imprinting issue again: whatever you grew up with was normal to you, even if that meant violent alcoholism and fried chicken at every meal.

You can blame and do nothing or you can make choices and move on, but you can't be un-parented, and there are no do-overs.

It's time to move in a positive direction.

I identified my negative imprinting and Chucked It! Now it's your turn.

We make choices every day, many without thinking, some purely reflexive and unconscious. But the conscious decisions, the ones we're wholly responsible for, are the decisions that provide the greatest opportunity to change direction, seize an opportunity and improve ourselves mentally and physically.

Good mental health follows a lifelong plan as well, though much of what we do mentally and emotionally is on a subconscious level. But we can all use fine-tuning, particularly when we realize that our problems are causing us to sabotage ourselves.

See a professional if you have issues that need addressing. Don't mask the pain when it can be alleviated with something as basic and beneficial as counseling.

Be cautious about self-help seminars. They often only skim the surface and fail to address the deeper psychological issues at hand. Self-help gurus abound, and they're mostly pushing simple ways we can motivate ourselves and take a step in the right direction, but they don't address the deeper problems. And once we're away from the seminar, once the excitement of the moment has worn off, we're back living in our rut again; we're looking for the next self-help fix.

They like to tell you how they became successful, and how with the power of positive thinking and some insider information, you can do the same thing with your life.

Here are some flaws in that premise:

First, not everyone has the same opportunities in life. Yes, we applaud the Horatio Alger stories of the boys from the slums who rise through the ranks and become captains of industry. Of course those stories are exciting, because it almost never happens that way. If it happened every day, those stories would be boring, and the path of these "against all odds" success stories might not work for everyone, or even for most people. Most successful people have had a mentor, a fortuitous turn of events or just the right set of circumstances in which they were able to prosper.

And generally, the people behind those success stories have worked hard, with no short cuts.

Second, positive thinking without positive action is meaningless. There is no shortage of cheerful, optimistic and well-meaning people who have never fixed anything about themselves or sought to achieve anything. They are effortlessly happy and upbeat people, which makes them enjoyable to be around, but not particularly useful role models if your goal is self-improvement.

Lastly, the only goal with many of the people who would sell you a quick fix is getting your money, and getting themselves more money in the process. (And them getting more is significantly more important than *you* getting more.) Knowledge is power, and their wealth signifies to us that they have knowledge that we don't, and therefore, they have the power to empower us.

But money is in the hands of a lot of fools and charlatans, and wealth doesn't necessarily represent wisdom, nor has it necessarily been earned.

If something sounds too good to be true, it usually is.

And we all know, at least in theory, that money can't buy happiness but often, it's a motivator in our endeavors rather than us doing the endeavors for their own value. Granted, no one shovels manure for the joy of it, and some jobs have no joy except the money (though manure-shoveling money probably doesn't make *too* many people ecstatic). But chasing money is a sure way to unhappiness.

Study after study shows that people with money have the same incidence of emotional and physical problems as people with no money.

You are now entitled to ask, "Why should I listen to someone with money when he tells me not to chase money?" Because I didn't become wealthy as a goal; in fact, I continued to live a very frugal existence for years after I was a success, and continue to live a lifestyle that's quite simple compared to the average suburban teenager. I don't own most of the popular electronic gadgets that most of you probably carry everywhere, and I only got a cell phone a few years ago out of necessity. I've learned to enjoy myself, but I'm not indulgent by any standard of the word.

I became successful by single-mindedly pursuing a goal of better EAP service for everyone in need. Becoming successful and earning money was a happy accident of aggressively pursuing a larger goal and providing people with a service that they needed.

Don't think you need money to be happy. Chuck that thought!

You can do the same thing with your life that I did, and if you think I don't mean that literally, feel free to start your own EAP service. In fact, a number of years ago, my company got a contract with a large paper company. One of their locations was in Kalamazoo, Michigan, and the fellow who was providing and servicing the EAP for that location called me, worried he would lose the business because he was a small proprietor, and I had far more resources.

"Good for you, not so good for me," Mike recalls saying to me at the time. Mike has always kept his EAP relatively small so he can keep the service personal. As a result, some businesses would opt to go with larger EAP providers in order to save money. It wasn't the first time he'd been outbid for services, nor would it be the last.

I understood that my gain was somebody's loss; that's how capitalism works. But I also wondered how I could I change someone's potential loss into a potential gain for everyone. So, I made a deal with Mike: he could keep the clients under my contract and work with me on other locations, and expand his business at the same time.

"It was unexpected," says Mike. "Chuck and I have worked together ever since. How many presidents of companies still do training seminars and meet with the people their EAP is servicing? Chuck understands that what we're really providing here is relationships, and not just a commodity. The other large providers simply don't see it that way."

Mike was able to stay in business and expand and prosper through the connection we had made, I was able to expand my business, and we've also become friends for past 15 years. I understood once I met him that Mike is a very good clinician and an ethical person, and in situations where it's possible not to end with a winner and a loser, I opted to provide a situation where both of us could prosper.

What's the larger goal you want to pursue? It's your life; you have the capability to determine your own path in it. Maybe your goal is to start your own company; maybe it's to become a painter. Maybe it's as simple-sounding yet unbelievably complicated as raising your children right and being a good person. (It's been said that brave men wish to improve the world and brave women wish to improve their families. I'm not sure which task is more difficult…)

These things can all be done if you know how to start, and no quick fix will provide the answers any more than a fad diet will make you healthy.

You are the pilot of your own life, and you are entitled to happiness. There's nothing noble in suffering, no benefit to anxiety and guilt, no refuge in drugs and alcohol, no prize at the end of life for having lived in selfless unhappiness. You can live a happy, healthy life if you're willing to clarify your problems, identify your options and develop a plan for improvement.

Make the choice to live a happier and more productive life, and allow those who are in a position to help you, help you.

Chapter Sixteen
Chucking Fear

You Never Thought I Would
Make This Into A Poem

Thank you
for giving us
the opportunity
to consider
your proposal
which has received
careful consideration.

We are sorry
to say,
however,
that we do not feel
it is suitable
for publication
on our list.

Sincerely,
the Editorial Department
at Nordic Press, Inc.

Two waves were coming toward shore and the bigger of the two, the male wave, said, "I don't want to reach the shore. I want to stay a big wave. I know who I am."

His companion, the female wave, said, "It's okay—relax. You're not really a wave anyway. That's only temporary state. You're just part of the ocean."

After hearing that, the big wave was able to relax, let go and become one with the universe.

I like that story, and sometimes people ask me whether it means that everything is transitory, that life is a temporary condition, that all our problems in the end are meaningless. Is the wave part of a greater consciousness that never ends but simply changes form? Will the sea continue churning after we're gone?

It's a very philosophical line of thought, and the short answer is:

Yes. We are all temporary.

If you don't show up for work tomorrow, the world won't stop. Nor will the sun refuse to shine after you're gone. Life is transitory and eventually, everything we've done and everyone we know will be forgotten. Those with a shortened sense of history are certain that there's no way future generations could forget Abraham Lincoln, or Michael Jordan, or Bill Gates. They're wrong. History is very long and we are a very short part of it.

I've always liked poetry, and I still remember reading Percy Shelley's "Ozymandias" in school, which describes the poet reading the base of a statue built to an Egyptian pharaoh thousands of years before, a man who had ruled people and lands as far as the world was known to him. The inscription on the statue bore the words, "My name is Ozymandias, king of kings: Look on my works, ye mighty, and despair!" Except the statue has fallen over and the desert has reclaimed all the land as far as the eye can see.

Surely Ozymandias achieved far more than we have. The fact that he could order people to build a statue honoring him says something about the power he had. Yet today, you probably can't find the *ruins* of the statue that Shelley saw two centuries ago.

Humans are one of the only species that has awareness of its own mortality, which is probably why we've created such an expansive and imaginative societal framework. If other animals knew their time was finite, we might be faced with competing civilizations of beavers or chimps or giraffes. The knowledge of death—whether we subscribe to a religion or not—makes us acutely aware of the time we have on this planet.

But you can't live a joyful, productive life in fear of death. In fact, you can't live in fear, period.

Chuck that fear!

Most of us don't dwell on mortality until we're old and then, we're constantly reminded of it. But many of us live in fear: fear of doing the wrong thing, of saying the wrong thing, of looking foolish, of failing, of being vulnerable or unattractive or "different" in some way.

We're all flawed. We all make mistakes. We're all works in progress and we all fail at times.

And none of us truly knows what comes next.

The old joke goes, "If you want to make God laugh, tell Him your plans."

Living in fear is no fun, and if you believe that there's a Supreme Being who cares for you and wants you to be happy, then surely He wants you to live life without fear.

Even if you don't believe in God, you're still entitled to a life filled with joy. You're here anyway—may as well make the most of the opportunity.

It's okay to not know what comes next, because the person who tells you he knows what's coming next isn't any more certain than you are. No one knows what comes next.

It's okay not to know.

In fact, the sooner you admit that you don't know more than you do know, the happier you'll be, because realizing that the vast majority of what happens around you is beyond your control can be very freeing.

When an executive at a manufacturing company we worked with unexpectedly died, I provided a group counseling session with the company's executives. One man, a senior engineer, nervously asked, "What do we do now? What direction are we going in? What's going to happen next?" Trained as an engineer, he wanted concrete answers.

"Right now, you don't have to know the direction," I told him and his co-workers. "You're not ready to know yet. You're still processing the loss and the grief. When you're ready to know, you'll see the direction things are going in, and that change will come, you can change it if it's not what you want."

That seemed to relieve them. They wanted an answer to an unanswerable question, and answering it or giving possibilities of what *might* happen wouldn't alter the future, nor would it have been honest. And honesty is the only policy.

"Sure, it's easy for you to say that it's okay to not know what comes next. You've already done something with your life."

True, but I didn't know what would happen when I went to Columbia University, and even though I was nervous, I wasn't going to pass up that opportunity. I might've failed. I also didn't know if my business would succeed, but I trusted that my idea, plus honesty and hard work, would equal success.

To this day, I'm never certain that all this won't disappear tomorrow. But I can live with that uncertainty.

And I certainly wasn't sure what would happen when I had to take a bus to the Golden Nugget on a hot day in a wool suit, with no prior understanding of the casino business. I had every right to expect to fail in that situation, but I didn't.

Had I passed up the chance altogether for fear of failing, I would have failed. Not trying is failure predestined. At least when you try, and you're trying something you actually *can* do, there's a chance you will succeed. (Conversely, there's nothing inherently noble in failing at something you absolutely *can't* do; identifying your strengths is an important part of setting and achieving goals.)

Will you succeed? If you commit to trying, you're ahead of everyone whose fear has inhibited them from even making an attempt.

Chuck that fear!

Okay, so you've committed to trying something. Maybe it's ambitious, like writing a novel or starting your own business. Maybe it's small and personal, like finding an hour every day to exercise, or eating better, or finding time each week to spend with an ailing friend or parent.

What will happen next? The future is unknowable. It's okay for you not to know what comes next.

The world we live in actually exists only in the present. The past is done and the future is unknowable.

So we should all live in the present. Actually, we have no choice.

We all know people who constantly regret the past as though that somehow alters it, just as we know people who perpetually fret over what might happen, as though they can control the future.

They waste the present—the only time they have truly to live.

Now, this isn't a nihilistic appeal to anarchy or free love or life without consequence. Part of living a whole life is taking care of those we care about, working hard and meeting our commitments. This is simply a reminder that opportunities, like life, are temporary. Seize the opportunity to take that class, or build your own business, or go to the park this afternoon with your kids. Live every day with the knowledge that the opportunities it presents may not be repeated soon, if ever.

When you're retired (if you retire), sitting in your rocking chair, what's more likely: that you'll recall how badly you sang on karaoke night in front of strangers, or how much fun you had that night when your friends talked you into grabbing the microphone? Will you relish the memory of not taking chances, of not talking to strangers, of not enjoying life's little moments when you had the opportunity?

We all fail and we all look foolish at times. Not only is it not the end of the world, it may be the beginning of something new. I once took the stage and performed standup comedy for twenty minutes, an experience akin to standing naked in front of an assembly hall. But I did it, I enjoyed it, and I'm glad I dared myself to try, because otherwise, I never would have known whether I could.

Knowing that I could, regardless of whether I ever do it again, was enough for me.

And in a million years, when we're gone, nothing will be remembered, and whether you stammered during your speech or your knees knocked during that audition or you were booed off the comedy club circuit, or even whether you got the lead in the movie and won the Oscar, none of it will be remembered.

So make choices that make you happy, take chances and move forward, and live life without fear or regret.

And if fear and regret dominate your life, talk to a counselor and address those issues so you can begin to enjoy the time you have and the opportunities before you.

Chapter Seventeen
Life Has Its Own Hum

Poem Crossing

Rushing,
you are late for a
meeting.

A poem crosses in front
of you?
Do you see it?

In the previous chapter, "Chucking Fear," we talked about worrying needlessly about the past, which is unchangeable, and the future, which is unknowable. All we have to live in is the present, and the present is the only reality we have the opportunity to shape.

So let's talk about the present.

The present can be frightening, too. No need to project into the future or regret the past when you're overwhelmed by the present. When I first moved to New York City, I was overwhelmed. The vastness of it, the busyness, the lunacy and foreignness were impossible to comprehend, and certainly beyond my control. I felt as though I was being swallowed up by this beast that was beyond my comprehension and control. And I was all about controlling things. Not that I was afraid of things that were difficult or new or strange, but I had never encountered something *so* big, *so* new and *so* incredibly strange.

I could've fought the sensation or I could have quit and moved back to Chelsea, but I was determined to not be deterred.

And gradually, I realized that I didn't have to control it—that I could be a part of it and participate and observe. Suddenly, the foreign aspects were enticing: what will a falafel taste like? And the people were just individuals who wanted the same things from life that I wanted, and that everybody wanted: shelter, food, security, companionship. And the city itself wasn't some gigantic monster about to swallow me up, it was a conglomerate of all these people and places and potholes and odd smells.

When I stopped trying to control what was beyond my control, I began to love New York City, and I embraced the diversity and strangeness and vastness of it all.

I Chucked my control and let life move at its own pace, and I fell into my own rhythm among the millions of other rhythms that engulfed me.

You don't need to live in a large city to feel engulfed or overwhelmed. You can be overwhelmed working in an office with four other people, or when taking care of your children, or when trying to balance your grades, your girlfriend and playing football. Being busy is hard enough, but controlling everything will inevitably overwhelm even the strongest person.

We sometimes are so intent on focusing on what we must do and what we want to do, most of which is completely beyond our control. The wants of the Earth's seven billion other human inhabitants and the whims of a universe that operates oblivious to our intentions continue all around us.

There isn't always time to smell the roses, but there are roses and opportunities aplenty.

Do you move with life's rhythm, or are you fighting the current, constantly trying to control what's beyond your control and plowing ahead, oblivious to the realities placed in your path?

Chuck It! It's time to abandon the illusion of control and focus on what you can actually do. It's time to open your eyes to the possibilities of life as they float past.

I still find myself surprised by chance encounters and unexpected opportunities. There's no greater joy than meeting someone—or finding or hearing something—you didn't expect to find or hear or meet.

Allow yourself to be surprised by the little opportunities life throws at you. It's the closest any of us will come to those childhood birthdays or Christmas mornings when we were most capable of unreserved joy and surprise.

My close friend Jeff lived in my apartment building for a long time, and I always knew him as the guy who complained at tenant meetings. We always nodded in each other's direction but never spoken, at least in part because I sensed that I didn't want to know him.

But one day, by chance, we began talking and realized that our personalities were complementary in so many ways that we began working together.

After displacing Mike Finazzo's EAP, I developed a working relationship with him and become friends; similarly, meeting and working with Jeff wasn't something I sought. But both relationships, which were potentially adversarial, worked out quite well. Sometimes, life presents you with opportunities when you're not looking for them. It's your prerogative to plunge ahead, oblivious to the opportunities around you or to pause, smell the flowers, talk to the stranger in your neighborhood, extend an olive branch to a competitor, notice someone smiling at you, pet the cat... Maybe you'll be surprised and, sometimes, pleased.

Opportunities present themselves to you only if you allow them to. Don't be so consumed by the task at hand or by the thousands of tiny distractions that clutter your day that you don't see the opportunities as they appear.

Similarly, living in the present requires us to stop trying to control those unpleasant aspects of life that plague us.

You can't make the driver in front of you go any faster by honking your horn. You won't make the supermarket line shorter by shouting at the cashier. Life has its negatives, its unpleasant surprises and dark chapters, and while we may be better able to recognize these, we're in no better position to control their outcomes than we're able to control any other aspect of life.

Control over uncontrollable negatives can be manifested in so many ways. Maybe the easiest way to exemplify how these issues interfere with the normal flow of life, and how so many of us are plagued by the feeling of being out of control, is to discuss the ultimate inevitability: death.

I was working with the CEO of a corporation in Detroit whose employees had our EAP contract. He was in the process of moving his business to another state. It was no small task; he had to relocate a thousand people without interrupting his business's continuity.

Amidst the chaos of this enormous professional challenge, he was also faced with a personal crisis: his daughter had a brain tumor. His only time to catch a breath was when we had our telephone sessions. Initially, he was overwhelmed, because no matter how hard he tried to assist his daughter and at the same time make the move of his business go smoothly, he still got frustrated. Both his personal and professional lives were out of his control, and he was emotionally devastated not only by both problems, but by his inability to control either one.

Why? Because he was a decisive, intelligent person who ran his own business, who was accustomed to having his orders carried out, and neither of these crises would move at his desired pace or resolve themselves to his satisfaction. Even though he was accustomed to exercising control, he couldn't control these two situations, and the frustration was maddening.

Eventually, through counseling him, I helped him realize that he had to let go of his illusion of control and let both processes move with their own rhythms. He came to realize that doctors and modern medicine could only do so much to save a terminal patient, and that no exertion of his will would make a difference. Everyone dies, sometimes in tragic ways and at unfortunate ages—even those we care the most for, even those we would willingly die for, and that fact is beyond our control.

This is a very difficult realization for anyone, particularly someone accustomed to being in control and decisively making things happen. We talked…and talked, and I helped him realize that it was time for him to relax, take a breath and see the world differently.

Death has its own timetable, just as life does, and while the loss of a loved one is never easy, an acceptance of its inevitability, and our inability to control it, makes the transition easier. As orderly creatures in a disorderly universe, we fear death and resent its intrusion, and believe that we can somehow control it.

We can forestall it by eating right, exercising and not smoking, but sometimes, awful things happen to nice people, and the circumstances are completely beyond their control. Control what you can control: put on sunblock, don't get in a car with a drunk behind the wheel, don't play on the railroad tracks. But don't expect to cheat the inevitable, and don't believe that fervent hope outweighs physical law.

We encounter immutable laws that are beyond our control every day, but we tend to think of tragedies in philosophical terms rather than logical ones. Often, after a tragic accident, people will say things such as, "How could a three-year-old drown in a swimming pool? She was only alone for five minutes."

We want the theological answer, the comforting answer, and those are there for us as well. But the real answer is that despite our wishes that such things shouldn't happen in a just universe, most three-year-olds can't swim, they can't hold their breath for five minutes and they can't breathe under water. Therefore, unsupervised three-year-olds who can't swim will inevitably drown. It frightens and saddens and angers us, but the universe has its laws and its own pace, and wishful thinking won't alter those rules.

All the willful personal control in the world can't overturn physics. You may as well ask the sun not to set or the oceans not to be wet.

Life and death will move at their own paces. All we can control is our reactions to them: our embracing of the positive opportunities that life presents us with, and our acceptance of death's inevitability and all of life's other unwelcome changes. Life's essential nature is constant change.

Chapter Eighteen
Finding the Quiet Spaces

Present

You are here,
alone,
reading this.
Unlike any moment that has come before.

Feel that.
Take it with you.

Some of my favorite days in my life, the days I remember fondly, are the snow days when I was a kid. They were whole days with no school and nothing to do, and I knew the possibilities were limitless.

Did I network on those days to try to improve my financial standing in the world, or endeavor to improve myself as person? Did I study for school or get a head start on my summer reading? To be honest, I don't recall. I might have, but I doubt it.

I mostly did what kids like doing most on snow days: built snowmen, got into snowball fights, hung out with my friends, watched cartoons and read comic books. Snow days were an unexpected break in the routine, and as a kid, I knew how to use suddenly available, unplanned time: to amuse myself. And to this day, I love the memory of those days.

How do we as adults handle unexpected "free" time? I've heard people say all of the following:

"Young man, nothing in life is free…"

"You don't understand. I have *somewhere* to be."

"These delays are complete wastes of time."

We're so focused on constantly working and getting places and achieving things that many of us have lost our appreciation for doing nothing. Doing *nothing*, it would seem, should be easier than doing just about *anything,* but for some of us it's the hardest thing to do (or not do) in the world.

We're so task-oriented that some of us schedule everything, including bathroom times and intimacy. In fact, I was in a public restroom recently and the men on either side of me were working as they relieved themselves, receiving phone calls and texts and juggling their briefcases.

May I never be so busy that I can't find the time for an unscheduled visit to the bathroom.

The very nature of our culture is fast-paced, loud and assertive, and nowhere more so than the northeastern United States. Most of us are so accelerated through life that we even talk fast. For us, speed walking isn't exercise; it's how we get from place to place. We like to feel like we're getting things done all the time, multi-tasking and being Supermom and Superdad and priding ourselves on cramming far too much activity into too small increments of time.

I'll sleep when I'm dead, and lunch (to quote Michael Douglas in *Wall Street*) is for wimps.

And, as though we aren't sufficiently goal-oriented and constantly in motion, many of us have taken to creating, in our children, a race of junior-executive versions of ourselves. These are the kids whose days are completely mapped out, wholly structured and utterly joyless exercises in task completion. I've listened as parents have mapped out their children's days, and it typically sounds something like this:

"After school we go right to math club, and from there to soccer practice, and after a quick dinner it's time to practice the piano, then two hours of homework, then off to bed, where it starts all over again the morning."

Being goal-oriented is wonderful. I've always been goal-oriented, and I achieved my biggest goal and continue to expand and refine it, so I'm certainly not opposed to having determination, direction and a good work ethic. But in those early days, I also didn't have a lot of down time and quiet spaces, and my personal life suffered for it. I was always running, remember, and the perpetual motion was an avoidance device. If you don't slow down and you never rest, you'll never feel alone, and if you do feel alone, you might have to address the source of all those bad feelings.

But after therapy, I realized that I actually like being alone. For one thing, I'm pretty good company. (Such declarations are better left to others, but I know I enjoy being with myself, which is a good start.) For another, my alone time was a great opportunity to relax, or to think things through, or read, or just stare off into space.

I realized that every minute of my day didn't have to be visibly productive. I was allowed to rest and relax.

And I came to understand that daydreaming and relaxing were actually highly productive. Daydreaming leads to creative, unstructured thinking, and relaxing allows the brain to re-energize and refocus.

Doing nothing part of the time, in fact, helps me do everything else.

I'm still very determined and goal-oriented, but now I allow myself the space to do absolutely nothing at times, and I've come to appreciate that I'm actually better at working and reaching my goals with some quiet time every day. It gives me time for mental and physical recuperation, and for creative and relaxing thoughts to bubble to the surface of my brain.

How many times has each of us gone to bed with a dilemma or problem weighing on our minds, only to wake up to find the solution, or the anxiety gone? Our brains are wonderful machines capable of sorting through a great many problems, but only if we give them space to work. Sleep is a great space for unconscious sorting, but so is quiet time when we're awake.

Thinking and relaxing both require quiet time. A friend of mine who is a writer says that his kids often comment that they rarely see him actually writing; mostly, he stares off into space. "I tell them, I'm always sort of writing in my head," he says. "Only at the very end of it do my fingers need to do anything."

If you work and you have kids and you have a social life as well, the bad news is that there may not be a great deal of quiet time in your life now or in the foreseeable future, which is why you have to seize the opportunities when they arise, and create opportunities for yourself when you see an opening.

Don't allow modern "life" to prevent you from actually living.

Finding quiet spaces requires a different strategy for thinking about how we organize our time, because we've become accustomed to always talking or listening or having some sort of electronic stimulus in our ears and eyes. It requires finding literal quiet, if possible, and a quietness of the mind, whether there are unwanted intrusions surrounding us or not.

Finding quiet also requires a different view of obstacles. Most of what we consider to be obstacles or inconveniences are utterly beyond our control. All we can control is how we react to such things.

You can't control things that are beyond your control. The traffic jam won't break up any faster if you shout or honk your horn, and the plane won't leave the airport any faster if you shout at the flight attendant.

You can't even always control the things that are allegedly within your control. Your kids might still run wild in the store; the power may cut out in the middle of the meal you've been painstakingly preparing. You might get every detail in your presentation absolutely correct, only to have the hard drive crash on your computer.

Frustrating, yes, but not within your control. And not resolvable with a cascade of profanity, either.

You can strike up a conversation with the person sitting next to you. I've met interesting people, and even people who became longtime friends, by starting a conversation with a fellow stranded traveler. Even if the relationship goes nowhere beyond that initial impromptu conversation, it's human contact—something we all crave whether we're aware of it or not.

Read a book. Make some notes on where you'd like to go on your next vacation. Or just breathe deeply and stare off into space.

Teach yourself how to rest and relax. (Or have someone teach you; not everyone is as good at doing nothing as I am.) I take some time every day to meditate, and have done so for more than thirty years. It clears my head and helps me focus. I'm not seeking a transcendent state necessarily, or communion with God (though some of you may seek precisely that)—just a small amount of peace of mind in a cluttered universe.

"Chuck, I love being always on the go, being constantly stimulated and goal-oriented. Can my quiet spaces be noisier than yours?"

Of course they can! We're not cookie-cutter people. Everyone is unique, and if life feels good to you with constant stimulation, then find ways to use that energy to further yourself as a person.

For example: volunteer. For years, I've volunteered at an animal shelter, a truly selfish act on my part because I love animals. But you can volunteer to read to the elderly, or work in a soup kitchen, or coach Little League or pick up trash on the side of the road. Use that extra energy to make the world a little bit better.

Or, spend more time with your loved ones. Relationships require care and attention, so don't allow them to wither because work seems more important. The people you care for are always more important than work, and even though work helps you provide for the people you care about, that income is no substitute for affection and attention. Kids are only kids for a short time (I know, when they have colic or they're misbehaving, it seems interminable) and your relationship with your significant other got the whole process rolling, so he or she can't be neglected, either.

It needn't be all expensive vacations and dinners out. Just spending time with those we care about is intrinsically rewarding to all parties.

So how do you know when the job or the money has become more important than your loved ones? When you have sufficient money to buy them gifts out of guilt to compensate for the time you *don't* spend with them.

Chuck that habit!

Work hard and play hard. Reward yourself for how much you do by occasionally doing nothing. And don't just tell the people you care about that you love them: spend your time with them.

Actions truly do speak louder than words, and the greatest gift we give to anyone, particularly in this cluttered modern life, is our time.

Chapter Nineteen
A Business Plan for the New Millennium

The Old Piano

She told Janine,
who was six years old,
the piano was being sold
because
it was old
and
out of tune.

I watched her delicate body
quiver
as she asked her mommy
what will happen
when she
is no longer a child.

Where do we stand as a culture?

In some ways, it's the best of times. Our nation remains prosperous and productive, and in terms of *things* to distract us, we've never had more.

But there are aspects of our culture, particularly our business culture, which are sobering and even alarming. Many American jobs are being exported to countries where labor is cheaper; many working people can't afford insurance for themselves and their families; and many of us work longer hours with fewer vacations and less real money (wages adjusted for inflation) than our parents did. Millions of Americans feel overworked, under-appreciated and dissatisfied with the content and direction of their lives.

That dissatisfaction is reflected in the number of Americans who medicate themselves with drugs, both illicitly and legally, and the number who suffer in silence with debilitating emotional and psychological problems. As a culture, we have defined what it means to succeed and what it means to be happy, but too few of us can identify what "success" means; too few of us feel like we've made it, and not enough of us are truly happy.

The numbers don't lie when people report such things in polls, and I know what the numbers don't say, because I talk to people every day who work for a living: every statistic, every number that evinces our dissatisfaction with our lives is a real person.

When you see a headline that says, "Company X lays off Three Thousand Employees," it's a sobering reminder that in the corporate world, employees are sometimes seen as an expense—one that companies sometimes must limit in order to stay profitable.

Three thousand employees is a cold number, but as you learn in the EAP business, each of those numbers is a person with a family and friends and expectations for his or her life. Each one of those three thousand is that one man at Credit Lyonnais, feeling lost because his means of support and his identity have been assaulted.

I know I was naive when I went into this business. I knew nothing about running my own company and the business world cures naiveté quite quickly, usually in a painful fashion. When the director at Campbell Soup started a competing EAP and took the client for himself, I had to lay people off, renegotiate my lease on the office at 27th Street and 6th Avenue, stretch out payments over time and not take a salary for a year because I lost the big account. It was a painful experience, partly because I felt betrayed, but mostly because I had to let go of people I valued and cared about.

But in many businesses, the CEO and top people are protected when something like that happens. Employees get laid off or downsized, but top dogs never lose their secure spots in the sun.

No one can be so altruistic in running his business as to ignore the economic realities, or he won't be in business very long. But, I've shared in the pain during lean times just as I've shared the gain in prosperous times.

I've also had to fire people over the years; it's inevitable in business. Not everyone is a good fit for their job; not everyone will work hard, and some people won't work at all.

Just as I've never looked at EAP strictly as a commodity, I've never viewed my employees as mere debits or credits on the company ledger. Yes, it costs more to hire good people, but for the services we provide, I couldn't in good conscience hire anyone but the most qualified applicants. Yes, I pay more for them than does a company whose triage workers are essentially low-wage answering services.

I treat my employees well and reward them for their efforts. Many companies are always looking to rid themselves of well-paid, highly experienced employees with the mistaken notion that younger, lower-paid employees cost the company less money.

It's a misguided approach. Experienced people provide better service with less direction and with greater customer satisfaction, which leads to better customer retention, which invariably leads to a more profitable business. Well-paid employees don't leave your company as readily, and replacing them requires more hiring and training. Employees who feel appreciated tend to reward you in return for your rewarding them.

Maybe it boils down to having an optimistic view of human nature. A pessimist believes there are those who will cheat the system, and treats everyone accordingly. I believe the vast majority of people want to work hard for a fair wage and will reward their employer for how well they're treated. The cheaters are easy enough to spot and weed out.

I can't claim to be an expert on business (though I've noticed that most of the "experts" tout their immense financial gains and dismiss the human wreckage they've left in their wakes, as though the primary purpose of business is to benefit the few at the expense of the many). I've made business mistakes in the past, and I may make others in the future. After all, I came to be a businessman as a vehicle for providing people with the counseling services they needed, not by making money my primary goal.

Despite my lack of training and my initial naiveté, I've managed to build a business that services more than nine hundred companies that employ four million workers, and my company is the eighth largest of its kind in the United States. And it's the one of the few in the top ten that's privately owned. (Boards of directors and shareholders tend to make profit-driven decisions rather than quality-enhancing decisions.)

Not bad for a guy who couldn't get a client for his first nine months on the job.

I don't pat myself on the back to serve my ego. I know my way of doing business is the right way because every day I talk to people who are dissatisfied with the quality of their lives. Some of them are at the bottom of the workforce, struggling with lousy benefits and working jobs that treat them as just another part of the assembly line. Others I speak to have the high salary and terrific perks, big homes and expensive cars, and they're not happy either.

Is this truly the American dream?

I can only conclude from the results of my personal business venture that I was onto something from the very start. Again, in evaluating what I really wanted from life and pursuing what mattered to me, the path led me to some profoundly happy accidental results.

But running a business that's successful *and* one that treats its employees well *and* services its customers well? That's no accident. Those things occurred because the way I viewed this business incorporated the way I viewed life: that everyone deserves respect; that kindness and compassion should be cornerstones of every human interaction, even in business; that the I-win-you-lose model of doing business is wrong in terms of profitability and equitability; that my success didn't correspond with my competitors' failures, and that it could enable others to succeed as well.

The old way of doing things, the I-win-you-lose system that has money as its only bottom line, isn't the only way of doing business. In fact, it's not even the most satisfying or profitable way to do business.

Chuck that old system!

People who work hard deserve better, in every business and at every level, and people want more from their working lives than an unpleasant system where the employees are always suspected of cheating the system, clients are treated with disdain and CEOs are entitled to reap ridiculous profits whether their business model works or not.

Work should give our lives meaning. I realize that this is a modern view of labor because for thousands of years, work was only viewed as a necessity. Enjoying your job in those days not only wasn't a consideration; the likelihood of such a thing happening was absurd. In general, the only people who enjoyed their lives were the titled gentry who didn't work at all, having inherited their status and wealth. For everyone else, work was simply the means by which you stayed alive, justified your place on Earth and kept your children from starving.

But societies evolve, and just as we no longer put ten-year-olds in sweatshops or have bonded servitude, we now allow for ambitious self-invention, flexibility and ambition.

In pursuing my goal of creating an expansive and flexible EAP service, I wasn't so much inspired by the corporate robber barons I saw on Wall Street. I was more inspired by the guys pushing the food carts up 5th Avenue, who had come to this country not knowing anyone and not knowing the language; the ones who started their own businesses and found their way in the world's most dynamic and competitive city.

If they could succeed on their own terms, so could I. And so can you.

The changes in how corporate America operates must come from the top down, of course, but employees also need to realize that they aren't exploited and neglected without their consent. That realization is why unions were organized in the first place: so workers could demand equitable treatment. Employees still have the right and responsibility to demand better working conditions for themselves.

It's an old psychologist's axiom: no one can take advantage of you without your permission, and we have allowed ourselves to be squeezed into tiny cubicles, worked overtime without compensation, had our benefits cut and our dignity assailed.

In the United States, according to *The Economist*, business executives make approximately four hundred seventy-five times what the average worker in their business earns. By contrast, in Japan, it's eleven times as much; in Britain, twenty-two times; in France, fifteen times; in Mexico, forty times; and in Germany, twelve times as much. You get the idea. CEO salaries in our culture are ridiculously out of proportion to their subordinates', and very often, that CEO's leadership (or lack thereof) has no bearing on the success or failure of the company. And other cultures appear to recognize this fact.

Where does a number like four hundred seventy-five come from? We're often told that it's what the market will bear, but that disparity between top and bottom isn't necessary, particularly when those at the bottom are struggling to make ends meet. I'm not advocating socialism, and everyone should work for his money. But I've never heard of a job so vitally important that that one person's presence has the same value as four hundred and seventy-five of his or her entry-level employees.

Sometimes, as a culture, we reward the wrong attributes. Wealth isn't necessarily a sign of achievement (some people inherit or steal all their money), just as celebrity isn't necessarily evidence of talent. (There are too many examples of this to even begin mentioning them.)

Making a huge salary as the CEO of a successful company is an achievement. An even greater achievement is being CEO of a company where people are paid well and treated with respect.

How many stories have we read about CEOs and their companies that have that dynamic?

The corporate robber baron who buys assets and sells off their parts and makes billions in the process is the contemporary corporate role model. Very often, there's no value added in this CEO's machinations: the companies bought are liquidated, the jobs sent overseas; the remaining employees are rehired at lower wages, benefits are cut and families are relocated.

It's a real feel-good story…for the CEO. Most everyone under him suffers for his manipulations and greed.

Chuck that system!

We've been programmed to believe that employees abuse the system and must constantly be monitored and shepherded through their day. Any other system is counterintuitive. Surely more freedom, better benefits and fewer hours leads to less productivity, right?

Wrong.

My employees have a four-day workweek. Why? So much of life is preparation, and one less workday is one less day dressing, getting the kids to the sitter, struggling through a commute and then doing everything in reverse at the end of the day. Some days, getting to work feels like half the battle. And work is…well, work. It can be exhausting and frustrating, even when it's rewarding. So I cut everyone's hours without cutting their pay. The result?

Productivity went up!

I have happier, healthier employees, and I know they have solid family values because they actually share more time with their families. Vacation days are one month in addition to the regular holidays such as Christmas, Thanksgiving, Labor Day, Martin Luther King's birthday and other major holidays. And we have no sick days—if you're sick, you're sick; take the time you need to get better.

We also pay good wages, offer profit-sharing programs, child and eldercare assistance and benefits that we discuss with our staff so we can provide the right type of support. I couldn't offer these advantages to my employees when I started the business, but as soon as we had the assets, I did. Creating a healthier work environment was a priority for me, and I'm not the only one.

Other progressive companies have added free day care. The assumption is that such a benefit is extravagant, but productivity actually goes up! People with children miss a lot of work when their kids have snow days or school holidays, but with free day care, they show up more often, more work gets done, and they're happier. Again, it's win-win.

Some companies now allow personnel to work from home. With most corporate work accomplished electronically and over the phone, a commute is merely an exercise in frustration. But what happens when you have people who don't need to dress, battle the commute or be directly supervised? Again, the results run counter to our expectations, but more work actually gets done; the employees are happier, and it's a win-win once more.

We've worked under the old dysfunctional corporate model for as long as there have been corporations. As kids in school, we read about the robber barons of the Industrial Age, men who bullied and beat and sometimes even killed their workers, who drove competitors out of business, cornered markets, amassed fortunes and rode roughshod over everyone who got in their way. And we were told to believe that such business practices were not only unethical, they were antithetical to the American dream.

This is not how America should work was the implied message of those stories. And yet, many modern businesses run in very similar ways, and we celebrate those who exploit their workers and personally profit at the expense of their laborers.

Healthcare is no different. It's a dysfunctional system top to bottom, one that treats symptoms rather than the sources of problems, one that rewards treating people and their conditions as commodities and where denying care is integral to the culture. At every level, the system is flawed, and yet we cling to it because we believe we have no choice as a society.

The cost of healthcare continues to rapidly rise; malpractice insurance continues to rise; hospitals struggle to stay in business and to retain nurses; the cost of higher education continues to increase, causing potential doctors to think twice about bearing the cost of entering medical school; large public insurance companies are pressured by shareholders to increase profits by seeking ways to deny treatments, which then leads to patients failing to receive proper treatment, which sometimes leads to the patient developing even more serious illnesses; and experimental treatments are often not covered, which discourages innovation and risk-taking.

Our healthcare system should emphasize preventing disease and treating mental illness as a way of lowering overall healthcare costs, and we need to involve everyone, because health and wellness programs are only effective when participation is high. Many companies say that they have health and wellness programs but they fail to properly promote them, and the low participation leads to very little real effect.

The system is so broken, even our leaders don't know how to fix it, and the lobbies that would keep the status quo use the public's fear of poor care and higher costs to maintain the current system.

Chuck that system!

As a culture, we need leaders not of entitlement but of vision—men and women who lead with a goal of shared prosperity and kindness. The vast majority of the executive class in the United States does not currently take proper care of its employees and their families.

Years ago, I developed programs that focused on the importance of diet, nutrition, smoking cessation and weight loss. I also created mental health carve outs, which fully integrated third-party administrators with the existing EAP, providing better hands-on care. I also created patient advocacy programs to ensure that clients didn't get lost in the medical system. I did these things with the goal of providing better care, not more profitable care, and yet the result was that we had healthier and happier clients.

Creating an alternative to the status quo isn't hard and not only does it lead to healthier and happier clients, it's actually more profitable than denying care and scrimping on preventative care. In the healthcare field, we should ask ourselves the same question in every step we take: is the client better or worse for this? Because if the answer is "worse," the system is broken.

What kind of world are we creating? One where we claim to value all people, yet we use up and expend employees for personal gain. We live in a culture that claims to be spiritual, that says it values compassion and humanity above mere things, yet we disdain those who are downtrodden or exploited and idolize those who have accumulated wealth and power regardless of how that power and wealth were garnered.

You can build your dream, but with that dream comes a responsibility to your employees, and to humanity. I challenge business leaders to stand up and lead by using a methodology that promotes a better life for all, not just themselves.

Chuck what has been done by others! You don't have to work that way.

For me, it goes back to having a vision and being bold enough to pursue it. Not just a vision for what I wanted from life, but a vision of how that work could help others, and for humanity in general.

As Henry David Thoreau said in Walden:

We have professors of philosophy, but not philosophers. To be a philosopher is not merely to have subtle thoughts, but to love wisdom as to live according to its dictates, a life of simplicity, independence, magnanimity and trust. It is to solve some of the problems of life, not only theoretically…but practically.

We are our brothers' and sisters' keepers. Yes, we are a family—at work, at home and in the world at large. It's time we began thinking that way.

Excerpted e-mail correspondence at Charles Nechtem Associates, Inc.

Hello,

I'm thinking of extending the four-day-a-week schedule permanently. However, if we have a business office meeting or work-related travel, we will just have to make things work. Do we have enough people to make it happen? There will be no increase in office hours as I think we all know what we need to do to try to make the business successful. Five days is unhealthy; four days, I think, works better. No reduction in pay or benefits—and I am reviewing medical benefits shortly and would like input in this area.

Also, I'm not sure how much vacation time we're supposed to get but I think we should get at least get four weeks in addition to the regular holidays like Christmas, Thanksgiving, Labor Day, New Year's, etc. What does everyone think about that? (Twenty days, Twenty-five days…)

Any other ideas, please let me know.
Let's lead the way, setting the trend in business and life!
—Chuck

Hi, Chuck,
I like that you are leading the way in balancing work and life. It's nice to practice what we preach. I believe we have already seen how the four-day workweek benefits all of us. No one has called out sick in our department. It is important that we feel we have input, so I appreciate that you are asking for feedback. I believe four weeks' vacation is fair. Four-day workweek, four weeks' vacation, 401(k), fabulous benefits—who wouldn't want to work for this company! Ha.
—Sue

Hi, Chuck!
I have found that having four-day weeks has relaxed me more. Yes, it can sometimes get CRAZY busy but as long as we all do what we are supposed to do in the office and not slack off, it can work well. I also like the idea of having more vacation days. I don't think anyone will disagree with the idea. We just need to make sure that we work our schedules around each other, especially when someone needs to travel for business.
Regarding our medical benefits, I would like as much information as possible because, as you know, I will need surgery in the near future, so I need to ensure that I won't have any problems with coverage.
Thank you for your generosity. I feel at ease knowing that we have a boss who wants our input and respects our opinions.
—Ivette

Chapter Twenty
A Passion Quest

Hunter at Penn Station

It was sometime in mid-October.
The October after Sept. 11th, 2001.
I went to Penn Station,
to buy a ticket for the Long Island Rail Road.

Along the wall next to the ticket booth
Were the photos of some 500 people
Missing, and presumed dead from the World
Trade Center disaster.

I took some time to read the messages
One I remember
Was about a woman
Her first day of work on the 98th floor.
She was 32 years of age
And her name was Zhaneta Tsoy.
I wrote her name down
To keep it with me.

There are other photos of people smiling
with their children, spouses, friends, pets at their side
All so full of life in the moment.

Overwhelmed, I went to lean against the post,
Let the crowd pass by
And just stand there.
Suddenly, I felt a tapping on my back
I turned around
And I saw a young boy, maybe 8 years old.
"You're Hunter's friend," he said.

Not sure what he meant
He said again "You're Hunter's friend,
Hunter; the dog at the Jersey City Animal Shelter,
you know he's adopted now?"
"Yes," I said.
"I know he is adopted."
"I saw you at the animal shelter take Hunter for a walk
And you know what? Now I walk the dogs too!"

"That's terrific, thanks for saying hello."
I shook his hand and told him to keep up the good work,
Watched him smile brightly and walk away.
I had never seen him before.
But in those few moments with all those photos
There was a juxtaposition of feelings
And I understood a little more about this lifetime.

When I first got the idea for this book, I thought I would simply be writing about my ideas for how a business should ethically and conscientiously operate. And I was, initially, but the more I thought about what the book should be about, the more I realized that the ideas were applicable to life in general and not just to the business world, and that they could be beneficial to most people, even those with no interest in starting a business or taking personal risks.

The interconnectedness of people—our need to be heard and to hear each other—is innate, and our acts of compassion, generosity and kindness have ways of creating ripples in the larger community.

The story told in "Hunter at Penn Station" is true, for example. Amidst all this overwhelming grief, the chaos and uncertainty and sadness that followed 9/11 that affected so many of us as individuals and our collective psyche as a nation, I had this glimmer of hope and joy. Here was this small boy, inspired to volunteer at the animal shelter by what he'd seen someone else doing.

I volunteer at the shelter because I love animals and because it gives me joy. It's a truly selfish act, but by doing this selfish act, I had accidentally inspired someone else who then might tell a friend, or teach his children, or spread this act of kindness in unimaginable ways.

I realized, from that chance encounter and others, that random acts of kindness and consideration are rarely isolated acts. They spread. The Buddhists call it karma, the belief that one's positive actions are in some way returned, but I understand it as something more vast than a mere series of personal interactions that benefit us as individuals. The universe has karma, and our acts of kindness and consideration have ways of spreading and reaching people we'll never even know.

And if incidental acts can have this effect, what effect do deliberate attempts to improve the world have?

I built my business backwards, like the way I've lived my life—pursuing worthwhile goals and creating opportunities because they mattered most to me. I learned how to build a business that makes a difference by accident, but in imparting what I've learned, my motives are quite deliberate.

It's time to build a better model for modern life.

My friends sometimes laugh at me because I love to ride the bus and the subway. (I'm in good company, because so does billionaire New York City Mayor Michael Bloomberg, whose family, like mine, lived in Chelsea.) Sometimes, I ride the bus from La Guardia Airport (the #60) to the subway through Queens, into Manhattan and then to the PATH train in Jersey City, where I live. In Sarasota, Florida, I often take the SCAT bus from the airport.

I can afford taxis or limos, but I love to look at the faces of the people on the bus and subway. These are the people who are just making it—and some of them aren't making it. But despite the obvious difficulty of their lives, I can see hope in their hearts and in their eyes. Many are new immigrants who board the bus with their children, their groceries as well as their hopes and dreams. They're cheerful and they're optimistic, but they're struggling to get by, never mind get ahead.

I know from my own modest beginning that dreams take time to build, but I believe it's our job to share them and help to make life better, which means taking care of everyone like we're all family.

To some people, that idea sounds dangerously socialist or incredibly naive, but we live in the most affluent country in the history of mankind. If we can't muster the will and resources to care for all of our society's members, then no one can.

I see that there are just as many searching and frustrated faces on airplanes and in corporate board meetings as hopeful ones. These people aren't poor; they haven't been denied access to the dream; but they're still unsatisfied with where they are and what's required of them to stay there. They actually look unhappier than the poor people—maybe because they've worked hard, they've had goals, but life has weighed them down, and they're still unhappy.

Their unease is different than that of the poor, struggling immigrant, but in a way it's worse, because by any definition, they have achieved the American dream and they *still* aren't fulfilled.

They're part of our family, too, and they also need our help.

I had one recent caller to our employee assistance program who told me that in the past three years, she had been on six different types of medication to address her anxiety. She said her mother had died when she was fourteen, her father had been physically and verbally abusive, and she was the youngest of five children. She was five feet tall, one hundred twenty-five pounds overweight and never exercised.

"Are you receiving any counseling to address your anxiety?" I asked.

"No, the doctors are just trying different medications to see what works," she replied.

Anyone with her upbringing would suffer anxiety and depression. That's understandable, and because of those unresolved imprinting issues, her life has spun progressively out of control. In my mind, she represents our culture as a whole: anxious, depressed, not getting enough healthy exercise, eating to fill an emotional void, self-conscious, unhappy…and reaching out for someone to talk to and ideally, for some help in fixing her problems.

And the medical establishment's answer is pills to mask the symptoms rather than counseling to address the problem.

I told her we needed to create a new and healthy way of eating for her and an exercise habit that would make her feel good, both physically and psychologically; she would also need regular counseling. I also told her that this program would take time, but that it could quite possibly be much more effective than a bathroom cabinet filled with medications. I listened to her story, encouraged her to move forward and put her on the road to a healthier lifestyle.

As satisfying as it is to help someone address their problems, a much larger problem nags at me.

What about her peers, the millions of American suffering with the same, or similar or even worse problems? Who are they talking to, and are they talking at all? What if their insurance doesn't have an EAP that provides such services, or they have an EAP that denies them coverage?

What if they don't even have insurance? What if they have no recourse but to live their entire lives as physically and psychologically unhealthy people—depressed, addicted, self-destructive, hopeless? Can we live with ourselves as a culture if we allow such people to fall through the cracks? If we allow them to live lives of unhappiness because we lack the will (and it's purely will, because we have the resources) to help them?

We're better than that as individuals, and we're better than that as a society. Or, at least, we should be.

We need to create a new protocol that, through counseling, addresses these early issues and how they relate to the present. We need psychological interdiction, not at the point where people are chronically depressed, anxious and addicted, but at an early age so these bad experiences don't manifest themselves later, growing into multi-headed, out-of-control emotional problems.

For those who would tarnish such a solution as economically unfeasible, the numbers are clear: it costs less money to educate a child than it does to keep him in prison. It costs less to provide counseling for a child than it does to put her through rehab. It costs less to teach a good diet, regular exercise and setting worthwhile goals than it does to send someone to a "fat farm," or to medicate them for the rest of their sad, anxious life.

It's not just about dollars and cents, of course, though there are those people, like the ones who run EAPs purely for profit, who would attach dollar amounts to intangible assets like good mental or physical health. Such attitudes are cynical, cold and morally wrong.

Chuck those attitudes!

Not everything has a subjective value—though when it comes to health, it's true that an ounce of prevention is worth a pound of cure, as the old saying goes. And that's as true of psychological well-being as it is of physical well-being.

When I was little, there was a song my mother used to sing: "He's got the whole world in his hands, you've got the whole world in your hands, we've got the whole world in our hands…" There were a lot of other songs about changing the world for the better. (It was the Sixties and for a while, it seemed that average people truly believed they had the ability to change the world for the better.) But even though those songs seem quaint and those days are long gone, I still believe we can change the world.

It won't be with grand gestures or revolution. We can begin changing things in small ways, wherever we are and whoever we are. As Mother Teresa said, "Do not do great things. Do small things with great love."

These aren't just nice sayings or church homilies. Creating a culture that addresses people's emotional and psychological issues, that provides equitably for those who work hard, that cares as much for the disadvantaged as it does for the advantaged, requires implementing plans and following through on them. It requires plans that provide access to a better life for everyone.

I challenge those who lead and those who would lead to set policies that enable every American, not just the few and privileged, access to the physical and mental assistance they need, to stop pretending that people's health is a bottom-line only issue, that we can afford missiles but we can't afford counseling for everyone who needs it.

It's time in America for leadership that truly leads and doesn't accept the unacceptable status quo, for those who would unashamedly express concern for those among us who have the least, and for those who need help most. (They're not necessarily the same people.)

Chuck that old system!

It's time for all people to take a stand and demand what we need, time for all of us to create a revolution of compassion, to place ourselves firmly on the side of what's right and demand a more compassionate system of caring for the body and mind, from cradle to grave.

And you will play a part...

Chapter Twenty-One
Be a Poet in Your Business

Where's Home?

Where's home
was the question.
"I reside in Jersey City,
although my home
is
wherever
I am."

Some of you are probably wondering what it means to be a poet in your business, so I'll explain the notion, although the way I run my business is probably the best example I can present.

Being a poet has developed a negative connotation in recent years, probably partially due to all the pale, sensitive singer-songwriter types whose album covers show them leaning listlessly against trees or staring wistfully off into the distance. There is an aspect of being a poet that requires stillness, quiet observation and sensitivity to others, but those are positive attributes, regardless of the negative stereotyping. And there's much more to being a poet than that.

A girlfriend gave this to me thirty-two years ago, and I've held onto it since. It's a letter from the poet Rimbaud to a friend:

> Self-knowledge, entire, that should be the first study of the man who wants to be a poet; he seeks out his soul, inspects, tempts, and teaches it. Once he knows its workings, he must cultivate it. That sounds easy, a natural development takes in every mind. There are so many egoists who proclaim themselves authors and a lot of others who credit themselves with intellectual progress... You have to be a seer, make yourself a seer. The poet makes himself a seer by a long immense and reasoned process of disordering the rules of the senses. All the forms of love, suffering, madness, he personally seeks out and exhausts himself of all the poisons, to save and keep only their quintessence.

In my own way, I accidentally followed Rimbaud's advice and took the whole of the human experience upon myself, absorbed it and learned from it. Living in New York City, helping people with problems and observing humanity's quirks and problems with a nonjudgmental eye helped me to become more empathetic. Yes, it's the nature of psychologists to be empathetic, to listen to the problems of others. That empathy can be taxed until a person is burned out or hardened, but it had the opposite effect on me.

I built my business by being accessible to people in need, but I never felt burdened, which is why I still counsel callers on a regular basis. As long as I have a way to help people, I don't feel burdened or overwhelmed when dealing with their problems; I have something to offer to remediate the problem and a great satisfaction in helping people turn their lives around.

And it's a fallacy that poets are inherently dreamy and lazy. It takes hard work to make something beautiful seem effortless to the casual observer. I'm reminded of John Keats' "Ode to Indolence," a celebration of laziness that he probably toiled over for weeks until it felt precisely right. Writing poetry can be hard work, but then doing anything that's truly satisfying generally requires genuine effort.

There's an accepting quality to being a poet, an understanding that the mistakes and blemishes and flaws are part of every person, every process and every thing. When we become judgmental rather than compassionate, we're not only not poetic, we cease being useful to each other. We may feel morally superior but in doing so, we alienate ourselves from humanity. Humanity is messy and makes mistakes. It's part of nature, just as it's part of our nature to seek improvement and orderliness.

Whatever your religion, it's easy to admire a man like Jesus, who spent most of his time healing the sick and counseling beggars and prostitutes. Healers go where healing is needed, not where it's comfortable or convenient, and they recognize that even though humans are imperfect, they're still deserving of love and care. Poets recognize the imperfect among us as brothers in humanness.

Part of understanding ourselves and human nature in general means accepting the mistakes and flaws, and encouraging ourselves and others to build lives around our strengths and achievements and not our flaws and failures. There's nothing wrong with failure if you've truly tried and there's nothing wrong with dreaming of unlikely achievements as long as you're working hard toward achievable goals. Reach for the stars, but first give yourself the opportunity to succeed!

Those are the keys to what it means to be a poet in your business: hard work and determination, empathy and compassion, acceptance and the setting of achievable goals.

Corporate America could run quite efficiently on these principles, but the majority of businesspeople have determined that it's more cost-effective not to, and the vast majority of the workers have quietly acquiesced to this terrible model. There are poets in the business world among us, but they're often overshadowed by the robber barons.

I don't just run my business as a poet; I engage my community in the same manner because positive civic actions are also part of building an ethical business. We operate EAPs all over the United States, but we don't operate in a bubble. I had other options, but I chose to locate my business headquarters in downtown Newark, New Jersey. It's a place that most people shun, as it never recovered from the riots of the 1960s. But amidst the social problems every big city faces, I see the same hope and determination I saw growing up in Chelsea or living in New York City: working-class people who are struggling, yet they're working hard and driving toward the American dream. I get on the subway with them and I talk to them every day, and while some people choose to despair over Newark's problems, I see the promise.

My company, in addition to the more than nine hundred companies we serve nationally, has contracts with the Newark Board of Education, the Newark Museum, the city of Newark and a company called Programs for Parents. With the Board of Education, not only do we provide the counseling services for all the employees and family members; we also provide a mentoring program for students and faculty.

As psychologists and social workers, I believe it is our responsibility to take the lead and offer services that can benefit our community. With Programs for Parents, we again provide the much-needed counseling services but also design special programs on such subjects as money management, business protocol and etiquette, as well as goal setting and career development. With the city of Newark, which has gone through a recent restructuring, I volunteered our business to contact every laid-off employee to determine if we could assist with additional support services, whether it's job training, resume writing, or financial or psychological assistance. It makes more work that isn't specified in our contract, but it's the right thing to do.

Our job is to empower people wherever we meet them, including the families of our hometown and every other place we offer our services. Newark is making a comeback; new mayor Cory Booker is making inroads in turning a big ship around, steering the city into a positive era of growth and development, and we want to assist with charting that new direction. It's a challenge, but it's an invigorating one: developing a new attitude and new empowerment will strengthen individuals, families, the city, the state and the nation, and we're up for the challenge.

Our efforts, person by person, will restore people's dignity, help to reduce crime, develop a better educated populace and produce citizens who can enjoy this life on earth and who contribute to society. When we're not downtrodden, exhausted, fighting to keep our heads above water financially and juggling obligations from work and home life, we can better take part in the system of government that our forefathers wanted for us.

It's not enough to want change and it's not enough to talk about what needs to be changed. Life doesn't exist in theory, so we're working to affect real change in the community around us.

Thomas Jefferson defined them as "inalienable rights" in the "Declaration of Independence"—that is, "life, liberty and the pursuit of happiness." My company is a means of assisting people in achieving those goals, and nothing gives me greater satisfaction than seeing someone who has realized that American dream, particularly when we've been able to help them.

That's the poet in me talking. But the poet in me *does* things that matter as well.

I've realized over the years that I would do what I do for no pay if necessary. (I know, successful businesspeople like to say that all the time, but in my case, it's true.) I do, in fact, provide personal services all the time—on planes, buses, subway cars, sitting in the park. It's my nature to be inquisitive, and it doesn't take much prompting for most people to talk about themselves. If I can assist someone with my counseling skills in my spare time, why not do it?

Sometimes the advice or corrective is quite simple, but because individuals are close to their problems, they sometimes fail to see the obvious. I often equate my job to that of a professional basketball coach: the players know how to play, but the coach is watching and listening, and when the team is out of sync he calls a timeout and reassesses the strategy, or creates a new strategy and gives the group the confidence to tackle the task at hand.

That's all counseling is for many people: a time out from the play, a fresh perspective to assist them in understanding what's happening and create a new strategy. We use our psychoanalytic skills and work behaviorally to make this happen—and it's invigorating when it works.

You're rightly thinking, *But Chuck, I'm not a psychologist. I can't fix people's problems.*

You have more power than you know. You can listen. You can give sound advice. You can advise others to seek counseling, or drug interdiction or whatever the proper remedy is. You can talk to your loved ones so you all understand each other a little better. Each of these activities requires only your time, attention and compassion.

In your business, as in your life, you can give your time, attention and compassion. You can't be available for everyone every minute, but you can provide others in that capacity. (That's what EAPs are for.) You can provide sufficient benefits so your employees aren't hurting physically and psychologically. You can provide adequate pay so they're not neglecting their children, working a second job on the weekend or struggling to pay the rent every month. You can give them adequate vacation time so they're occasionally refreshed. And you can listen to their concerns and address problems, whether personal or across the company, so your workers know they're valued. Remember, happy employees show up on time, are more productive and don't quit.

How much is that kind of corporate culture worth to you?

This isn't to say that you should defer important decision making to the whims of your employees. A bankrupt business benefits no one. Problems must be addressed and unproductive personnel must be corrected or let go. But it is possible to run a business that's both goal-oriented *and* empathetic; those goals aren't mutually exclusive. They're wholly complementary.

Cynics say that familiarity breeds contempt, and I know a lot of managers and CEOs who operate with this dictum in mind: if my employees are too comfortable with me, they'll abuse my good nature, and the company will suffer.

Chuck that notion! Familiarity breeds comfort, and comfortable people are happier and more productive.

The poet in me sees not just the beauty in humanity but the flaws, and understands that no person is perfect, and that no system with people in it can be perfect either. But I've run my business as a poet, with empathy and compassion balanced with determination, and I know it works not because I'm an idealistic dreamer but because I'm a realist who backs up his rhetoric with real experience.

In the traditional success story, the CEO tells you how the system works.

I'm telling you how it could work differently, and better.

Chapter Twenty-Two
Your Mission

Your Poem Here

The beauty of art is that it communicates something. This is my story, but it's your book, and in this venture, this communication that has occurred between us, you're a significant player. (It's just the two of us right now, at least until you share this story with someone.) So please add something that's personal to you or about you in the space I've left above.

I hope my story has been inspirational, but more importantly, I hope that the inspiration stays with you. I'm not going to say, "If I can be successful, anyone can do it." It's not easy to identify want you want in life and achieve it, but it is possible. (It's the "possibles" in life that fill us with anticipation; surely one of the most fun emotions humans experience.) If you want your life to be more full and satisfying, if you have a vision of what you hope to achieve and the determination to follow through, then seeing you accomplish your goals would make me immensely happy.

More importantly, it will make *you* happy.

Recently I was on the #4 train in New York City and sitting next to me was a mother who appeared to be intoxicated, and she was yelling at her four-year-old daughter. She appeared to be poor, uneducated and angry. Next to her was a young, obviously educated and cultured couple with a son about the same age. We looked at each other, embarrassed and upset, as the mother, yelling, dragged her child off the subway. We all have an idea of what the future will bring for this mother and her daughter, and we can't fix every problem we encounter, but with positive thinking and positive actions, we can help.

I know what it's like to be that child. I grew up in the city of Chelsea, Massachusetts. It's only 1.8 square miles, the smallest urban city in the state, the city under the Mystic River Bridge, one of the poorest in the nation. But Horatio Alger was born in Chelsea and he had great aspirations, too. This is a spiritual call to arms: this nation was founded by revolutionaries and we now need to bring that revolutionary spirit back to this country with a new socioeconomic change. It all starts with one person—you—and it grows with your leadership. I firmly know we will make it happen.

My call to every one of you reading this book is to be like Paul Revere, the man who announced, "The British are coming! The British are coming!" Our call is just as important as Paul Revere's: a call to sustain a quality of life that honors all people…and all life.

I firmly believe we have the ability to improve the world, and that's not because I'm a starry-eyed dreamer. I've always believed it; I developed a life philosophy and business model that proves my belief is correct, and I'm determined to share that belief with anyone willing to listen.

We have to be our own leaders in changing the world, and we do that by making choices about our lives and vocations, about living healthy psychologically and physically. Healthy living means first helping ourselves, becoming more aware of those around us and helping our community and fellow people. I've always believed in educating people about mental health issues and giving proper support where needed. It is immensely satisfying to be an advocate for improving the lives of others. I set an example with the type of business I operate and give people opportunities for good jobs. They in turn can provide valuable services with their jobs.

I've done those things, and in doing them I realized that I'm not extraordinary, that these ideas can be used by anyone to improve themselves and the world around them. It's a lovely revelation, and one that only has meaning if others follow the example and endeavor to improve their lives and their worlds.

I never wavered from my passion quest, despite life's obstacles, and I'll continue to do my part to make the world a better place. Now that you know my story and you've heard my philosophy for a more purposeful and rewarding life—one that improves the lives of others—it's your turn.

Where do you start? I've outlined the essential steps below. Remember, everyone has different experiences and abilities, and not everyone will have the opportunity or ability to change the way their company is run. But we all have the power to improve ourselves, and we're all capable of improving the lives of those we encounter. And we can expand that universe as well, to include those we know and even people we've yet to meet. Think about your personal and professional encounters the way I do: to me, everyone remains that first client at Credit Lyonnais, an individual with specific problems, needs and abilities. How can I be a friend/confidante/mentor/parent to that person?

You have the power to affect others in a positive way!

Now, see yourself as that one man, the one at Credit Lyonnais, and realize that you are your own first project. You have specific issues, abilities and needs, too. (It's okay—we all do.) Only by recognizing those needs, issues and abilities can you begin to improve yourself and in doing so, allow others to assist you. Fixing yourself, or at least identifying who you are, is a challenging first step, but it's essential. Remember, we can't begin to make others happy until we've learned to be happy ourselves.

And from there, who knows? With the right approach, you might make a lot of people happy before you're through.

Chuck's Rules for Building a Better You (and a Better World)

1. **Your first responsibility is to get to know yourself**. What makes you happy, and when your behavior is negative or destructive, what causes it? Counseling with a professional therapist can help you identify what's right and how to enhance those aspects of your life—and what's wrong and how to fix it. This is the foundation of a meaningful life: only by knowing ourselves can we begin enjoy ourselves and each other.

Chuck regret, guilt and self-pity! Begin to experience life without the negative imprinting that's been dragging you down!

2. **Live mentally and physically healthy**. Psychological issues lead to unhealthy habits like substance abuse and overeating, which can in turn contribute to feelings of guilt and anxiety, and on toward a vicious circle. Learn how to eat right, get enough sleep and regular exercise, drink in moderation, don't smoke or use drugs, and learn to forget your mistakes and forgive yourself for making them.

Chuck self-destructive behaviors! Mind and body are forever linked and working together. Learn to treat yourself well physically and mentally! You can't easily love others until you learn to love yourself.

3. **Extend your self-love to the people you care about and who care about you.** Share time with anyone (this includes your pets) close to you and tell them and show them that they're important to you.

Chuck anger, forgive mistakes and make amends! Spend your life with people who give it meaning, and endeavor to give their lives meaning as well.

4. **Find work that gives you personal satisfaction and your life meaning.** Freud said that the only two things humans need are love and work. So finish your education (or educate yourself further if you need to) and find work that empowers and satisfies you. If your work doesn't satisfy you, research and discover a profession that is challenging and brings meaning to your life. Encourage and assist your co-workers and employees in finding the roles that suit them best.

Chuck chasing money and power! If you work only for the money, then money is all you'll take away from your work, and you'll teach your employees that same shallow ethic.

5. **Communicate**. Listen to people you meet, share your stories with others and extend your assistance whenever you're able. Have faith in the general goodness in people. Yes, this attitude sometimes meets with disappointment, but better to have a few doors closed in your face than to never answer the door for anyone.

Chuck going it alone! We are social animals and beneath every structure of society, our existence is built around communication. Talk *and* listen.

6. **In your professional life just as in your personal life, give others not only what they need, but what they deserve.** Pay people well, provide benefits that actually care for them and their families, and provide incentives for them to work hard. Make all your work a collaborative effort. The better you treat the people who rely on you, the more valued they'll feel, and they'll return your generosity of spirit with hard work.

You don't have to be a CEO! Provide for your nurses' aides, teachers, waiters and waitresses, cabbies, paperboys, laborers, the cable installer... Everyone wants to feel valued and deserves fair compensation.

Chuck greed! There's enough of every essential to go around in life, and it's your moral imperative to ensure that those who work for you get what they deserve. Unhappy and exploited workers give back as little as they feel they've been given.

7. **Give something back to the community.** Volunteer, give time or money to charities, serve on a government council or school board, pick up trash on the side of the road... You'll discover that the more you give of yourself, the better you feel about the world. Anyone can despair that things aren't right, but those who work for change, even the littlest changes, know for a fact that things can get better.

Chuck selfishness that benefits no one! Embrace a selfishness that helps everyone!

8. **Accept disappointment and failure as normal occurrences.** Most of what occurs in life is beyond our control. We're all sad at times, we all fail, we all get sick and everyone eventually dies, but what we do between birth and our final disposition gives our lives quality, and makes the lives of those we care for better. Use that time wisely.

Chuck the illusion of control! Live in the present, hope for the future and endeavor to make those things in life you can control the best they can possibly be.

9. **Live with more joy!** Find enjoyment in what you do both personally and professionally, with whom you socialize and with whom you love.

Chuck those things that bring you unhappiness! Find the career, the home, the friends, the relationships or the special places that bring you happiness and Chuck the rest. And when you find joy, share it with those you care about.

10. **Go forth and share the message!** Understand yourself, embrace a healthier way of thinking and feeling and of doing business, and move forward with a plan for personal growth and a healthier, more joyful world in general. It's in your hands, and every person who knows this is empowered to make a positive difference in the world in their own unique way.

Chuck the old system! It's time to embrace a better way of feeling, thinking, working, eating… Together, we can change the world!